How You Can Be Sure That You Will
SPEND ETERNITY
WITH
God

How You Can Be
Sure That You Will
SPEND
ETERNITY
WITH
God

Erwin W. Lutzer

MOODY PRESS
CHICAGO

To my sister Esther,
who, during thirty years of outstanding missionary
work in Africa, has had the priviledge
of explaining to many people how they
can be sure that they will spend
eternity with God

ISBN: 0-8024-2719-7

5 7 9 10 8 6 4

Printed in the United States of America

CONTENTS

$\mathscr{W}$ELCOME
TO ETERNITY

Five minutes after you die you will either have had your first glimpse of heaven with its euphoria and bliss or your first genuine experience of unrelenting horror and regret. Either way, your future will be irrevocably fixed and eternally unchangeable.

In those first moments, you will be more alive than you ever have been. Vivid memories of your friends and your life on planet earth will be mingled with a daunting anticipation of eternity. You will have had your first direct glimpse of Christ or your first encounter with evil as you have never known it. And it will be too late to change your address.

Two contrasting scenarios come to mind. One is the self-assured rich man who died and went to hades, where Christ said he "lifted up his eyes, being in torment" (Luke 16:23). All of his faculties were intact: he could see, feel, hear, and remember his life on earth. And even today as you read this book, he is still fully conscious, knowing there is no way out of his predicament.

The other picture is of the crucified thief to whom the dying Christ said, "Truly I say to you, today you shall be with Me in Paradise" (Luke 23:43). All of his faculties were intact too; and today he still enjoys the presence of Christ in Paradise.

Would you be surprised if I were to tell you that Christ taught that more people were en route to agony than destined for ecstasy? More will be in conscious anguish than in rapturous joy.

Is it possible for us to know in this life where we will spend eternity? Some think not, insisting that about all we can do is hope for the best and count on the mercy of God. After all, we are sinners, and God is holy. There are, the argument goes, too many unknowns, too many hidden premises, too many opinions. "Besides," said one man, "I can wait to be surprised!"

On the other hand, it would seem strange indeed if God were to keep us wondering, suspended somewhere between a flickering hope and a persistent doubt. If He is our heavenly Father as Christ taught, we would expect that such crucial information would be revealed to us. Thanks be, it has been.

Many good people will join the rich man in hades, not because they are rich but because they are good and are depending on their own goodness to save them. For all their sincerity, they will find themselves on the wrong side of heaven's door. Or perhaps they are counting on the mercy of God, not knowing that it is given only to those who meet an important requirement.

No doubt some surprises await all of us five minutes after we die; but it is much better to be surprised about the indescribable glories of heaven than the indescribable agonies of hell.

Be wrong about social security; be wrong about baseball; be wrong about your career choice; but don't be wrong about where you will spend eternity.

This book will lead you on a journey. We will discover why we can know, even now, where we will be after we have said our last words and breathed our last breath.

With your Bible in one hand, and your doubts and questions in the other, let us begin our journey.

CHAPTER ONE

THE TRAGEDY OF MISPLACED FAITH

Faith can destroy you!

As residents of Chicago, my wife and I clearly remember the Tylenol® tampering episode that happened here in 1982. You might remember that someone bent on random murder put cyanide in a few capsules. The poison did its work very well. One woman who bought her Tylenol from a drugstore near our church died within minutes after taking a single capsule. In all, seven unsuspecting people died.

Two unforgettable lessons emerged from this tragedy. First, *faith does not in itself have any special merit; it does not have the power to change the nature of a drug from harmful to helpful.* Seven people firmly believed they were taking medicine, not poison. But their faith did not save them. In fact, their faith killed them.

Faith is only as good as the object in which it is placed. Or, to put it differently, *what* we believe is more important than the fervency of our belief. That old cliché, "It doesn't matter what you believe as long as you are sincere," just isn't true, as the victims of the Tylenol episode proved. Better to believe the truth with trembling hands than to believe error with steady confidence. What you believe really matters.

A second lesson we must learn from the Tylenol episode is scary indeed: *Sometimes a false belief resembles a true one.* To the casual observer, the cyanide looked just like the Tylenol powder. The label had all the earmarks of being authentic, so there seemed to be no need to distrust the contents. The promise was that these pills would relieve pain, yet taking a single one brought death.

Christ taught that many people who have a strong and abiding faith will someday discover that their faith cannot save them. To their everlasting chagrin, they will live to see the door of heaven slammed in their faces. They will spend eternity on the wrong side of the celestial entrance.

Maybe we can best capture the feeling if we use a story from this side of heaven's gates. Imagine standing in a swamp while a rescue plane flies overhead. You wave your weary arms and moan, but you know that the pilot does not see you. You do not have the strength to walk to civilization, and because your sense of direction is confused, you would not know where to walk if you could. Since the other members of your party died when your plane went down in the swamp three days ago, you are completely alone.

You stare into the night, knowing that you must simply lie down in the mud to die. You long for someone to be with you, but you must bear your despair alone. Waves of fear dissipate the courageous thoughts you had yesterday. You have a burning fever, and now you hysterically wait for the end.

Translate that feeling into cosmic proportions. You see the inside of heaven, catch a glimpse of some of your friends, but are told by Christ that you are permanently disqualified. There is no second chance, no opportunity to return the next day with the right documents in your hands. You can't reroute your travel plans. You turn away, never to see heaven again. You stare into the darkness ahead of you, conscious that you are entering the realm of moral chaos, loneliness, and darkness.

The words of Dante, long since forgotten, flash into your mind: "All hope abandon, ye who enter here!"

I wish it weren't so. And I know you do too. Yet Christ taught that many who expect the gate of heaven to swing wide open will be shocked to see it swing shut on them. Their exclusion from His presence is final, personal, and eternal. The words of rejection that they hear from Christ will ring in their ears forever.

Let us hear it from the lips of Christ Himself:

> Not every one who says to Me, "Lord, Lord," will enter the kingdom of heaven; but he who does the will of My Father who is in heaven. Many will say to Me on that day, "Lord, Lord, did we not prophesy in Your name, and in Your name cast out demons, and in Your name perform many miracles?" And then I will declare to them, "I never knew you; depart from Me, you who practice lawlessness." (Matthew 7:21–23)

These people never dreamed that they would be banished by Christ. After all, they acknowledged Him to be Lord and served Him. They had a whole bag of spiritual experiences that ordinary people like you and me could envy. I get chills when I visualize their contorted faces.

These religious types did not lack faith; if anything, they had too much of it! They had the confidence that they would enter into heaven. To hear them tell it, you would think they had a reserved seat in the front row of the balcony in the celestial cathedral. And now *this!*

If you did a personal inventory, their profiles would prove that these were not halfhearted souls who mouthed a commitment to God on Sunday and then did their own thing during the week. They were the dependable people who kept the church doors open year after year. They did miracles in the name of Christ. They even cast out demons and performed a litany of wonderful works. They thought of Christ as their Savior, not their judge. These good people were fooled into accepting cyanide in a Tylenol capsule.

Of course, it's easy for us to think we know who the people are that Christ was talking about. The other day I heard a preacher on television talk as though God didn't do anything unless He consulted with him first (that's an exaggeration, but you get my point). He told glowing stories about his work among the poor. He described all of the miracles God seemed to be doing through him. Maybe it was all true; maybe it was all false; or more likely it was a bit of both. Safe to say, God is His judge.

Let's not misread Christ's point: He does not want us to think that only those who make extravagant religious claims will be deceived. His warning is more basic: *If the people who seem the most likely to make it will be shut out of heaven, then plenty of other ordinary people will have the same frightful experience.*

Many sincere people who are devoted to their faith, many who would never brag about their relationship with God, and many who just quietly believe and have good works to prove it—these, too, just might miss the heavenly kingdom.

I'm glad that Christ didn't leave us confused about why some people will find themselves on the wrong side of heaven's door. To keep us wondering would not have been kind, but would have left us with our doubts to brood over our uncertain future. What we need is light to find the right path.

Recently, I read about a very tired man who checked himself into a motel late at night. He peered out of the darkened window as he closed the shades, then sank into a deep sleep. When he awoke and pulled back the shades, he saw majestic Mount Rainier through the motel window. The mountain had been there all the time; it was there even in the darkness. But he couldn't see it until the light of the sun showed him where he was.

That's the way truth is. We can't make it up. We can't create it by sleight of hand. All we can do is discover it in the presence of God's light as revealed in the Bible. Just as the light of the sun can enable us to see where we are geographically, so the light of another Son (Christ) can help us see where we are spiritually. *And I believe He wants us to know whether we will spend eternity with Him.*

The purpose of this book is to help us understand all that Christ has done to make it possible for us to know where we are going and that we do have a place reserved for us in heaven. I believe that we can be just as confident as the early disciples that our eternal future is secure. Just listen to what Christ promised them:

> Let not your heart be troubled; believe in God, believe also in Me. In My Father's house are many dwelling places; if it were not so, I would have told you; for I go and to prepare a place for you. And if I go and prepare a place for you, I will come again, and receive you to Myself; that where I am, there you may be also. (John 14:1–3)

The New Testament invites anyone, regardless of his or her past, to have the assurance that he or she will be escorted by Christ into the glory of a personal, heavenly existence. It is interesting that Christ taught that only a few would take advantage of this offer. Before I explain why, let's hear Christ's description of the two roads that are going in opposite directions.

A FORK IN THE ROAD

Recently I was discussing the credentials of Christ with a woman who said, "I believe that there are many paths to God. People can come in their own way." I told her I wished that were true, but I was confronted with a choice —do I believe her well-intentioned opinion, or do I believe in what Christ Himself had to say? He was not as broad-minded as many of the gurus who occasionally make headlines.

Christ insisted that there was a narrow road that led to eternal life, but, in contrast, there was a broad road that led to spiritual death. Clearly, there are two separate gates, therefore, two roads and two very different destinations. Hear it in His own words:

> Enter by the narrow gate; for the gate is wide, and the way is broad that leads to destruction, and many are those who enter by it. For the gate is small, and the way is narrow that leads to life, and few are those who find it. (Matthew 7:13–14)

Visualize an expressway with several lanes of traffic. Each lane has its own religion, philosophy, and point of view. Popular culture today tells us that we can choose our own belief, church, or personal philosophy. We can even switch lanes if we like. Everyone makes it to the finish line; everyone has a good time; everybody wins. The fun is in the journey.

Of course, it is quite true that when you are on an expressway, it really doesn't matter which lane you choose. And, yes, you can switch lanes as often as you like. In the end, you will get to the same destination as the folks who are zooming by on your left or the slowpokes you are passing on your right. It's not what lane you are in, but the expressway you are on that determines your destination. Your lane is your choice. Your final address is not.

Now it gets tricky. According to Christ, this wide expressway, which is thought by many to be labeled "The Way to Heaven" is actually "The Way to Destruction." Even in the Old Testament we read, "There is a way which seems right to a man, but its end is the way of death" (Proverbs 14:12). The cyanide is labeled "Tylenol."

In contrast, Christ says that the way to life is narrow and "few are those who find it." Here there is only one lane of traffic. The travelers come in various shapes and sizes, but, as we shall see, they share a common core of beliefs. The lane is too narrow to accommodate a host of different opinions about religion in general and about Christ in particular. But I'm ahead of the story.

There are more people on the broad way than the narrow one. And if we are not careful, we will get the two roads confused. Just ask the people who expected to enter heaven but were told by Christ to leave. He consigned those otherwise good people to the same destination as those who "practice lawlessness."

No wonder that John Bunyan, in his classic allegory *The Pilgrim's Progress,* wrote, "I saw there was a way to hell, even from the gates of heaven!" And so there is.

THREE LANES ON THE EXPRESSWAY

There are many wrong paths to God but only one right one. We don't have to be experts in identifying all of the false paths, for, if we are observant, we will notice that, despite differences, they all have a common characteristic. Try to find it as I describe three lanes of the superhighway that is going in the wrong direction.

The Ladder Climbers

While riding on a plane, I had a conversation with a man who said to me, "My greatest fear is to stand behind Mother Teresa on the day of judgment and overhear the Lord saying to her, 'Lady, you could have done a whole lot more!'" This man was an achiever who was trying to climb a ladder to God, but he wasn't sure whether he had even made it to the first rung!

Though it has variations, you have probably heard it a dozen times: God has given us a conscience, a moral nature that can distinguish (however imperfectly) between right and wrong. He gives us the ability to do good works that have the power to purify the soul. Our task is to use these gifts to the best of our ability.

Devotions, prayers, and disciplines help lift us rung by rung. And though we might not do all that we should, we can depend on God's grace to get us the rest of the way. As the cliché says, "God helps those who help themselves."

Chances are your friends believe this. Maybe you do, too. If you are a perfectionist, or if you have had to work for everything you have ever had, this route will be particularly appealing. According to a Barna Research report, almost all Americans believe they are good enough to get to heaven. That doesn't mean they think they are perfect, but that they think they are as good as, or better than, others. Even those who don't go to church see themselves as decent enough to have a good chance of "making it."

I often ask people this question: "If you were to die today and God were to say to you, 'Why should I let you into heaven?' what would you reply?" Nine out of ten say something like this: "I'm a pretty good person, and I'm trying hard to do better."

For now let's just file this answer in the back of our minds. We'll reflect on it later.

The Religious Types

Perhaps you are surprised that I've put religion in the "mistaken" category, that I'm listing it as just another lane on the broad expressway. "After all," you might say, "if religion does not get us to God, what will?"

But think about this for a moment. The people who were banished by Christ were certainly religious. I get the impression that they didn't just serve God occasionally but actually made it a way of life. When they were knocking on heaven's gate, the reason they expected to gain entrance is that they had done so many religious works in the name of Christ.

Religion can take many forms. For some, it involves sacraments, which are believed to be channels of grace for the faithful. The church, the argument goes, has the power to complete our incomplete deeds.

For others, religion is studying the ethics of Jesus and trying to live by those precepts. Knowledge linked with proper motivation helps us live a religious life, we are told.

We've all met those who believe they have met God through nature. The contemplation of the works of God leads to a knowledge of God, they say.

As you well know, there are dozens of different religions in the world, and each has its own creeds, ethics, and expectations. Religion, if understood broadly, is much more diverse than most people realize.

However, religion is really just another version of the "ladder theory." Religion defines the rungs more carefully and states the expectations more clearly. And, of course,

God's help is often sought. But religion, as such, is not the way.

Reasons will be given later.

The Mystics

Of course the mystics are religious too, but I've given them their own category because they are unique people who usually seek God with more intensity than others. Throughout the years, some devout souls (bless them) have renounced the world and secluded themselves in monasteries to find God. Maybe there are not many people who do that today, but the idea that we can find God within us through meditation and concentration is gaining adherents.

I've often admired the Christian mystics, those hearty souls who can take their faith that seriously. These men and women took the words of Christ "You shall love the Lord your God with all your heart, and with all your soul, and with all your mind" (Matthew 22:37) as their compelling vision. They fasted and they prayed; they meditated on the Scriptures or other devotional literature. They tried to deal with the sin that cropped up in their own hearts so that they could love God with pure motives.

Certainly some mystics found God, but not in the way or for the reasons that they thought. The temptation was to fall into some form of the ladder theory, to strive within the soul to make oneself worthy of God. Finding salvation through mysticism was such hard work that few mystics knew when they had finally made it. Indeed, most thought one could never know.

New Agers of today are into a different kind of mysticism, a form of spirituality that seeks an inner encounter with whatever God or gods there be. Techniques of meditation and self-help promise that God is just waiting to be discovered. Usually the goal is to lose one's identity and "become one" with the ultimate, or the divine.

These folks believe God is accessible to anyone who seeks Him. Often they also believe that He can be found in any one of the religions of the world. After all, if God is within us all, He is available to everyone, at any time, anywhere. We just need to find the key, and the door to spirituality will swing wide open.

But, as we shall see, the door is jammed.

SWITCHED SIGNPOSTS

Certainly these lanes on the expressway look as if they might be right. If salvation (that is, being reconciled to God) does not come by my striving to make myself a better person, what is left? What could appear to be more right than the view that we accept God's grace to do the best we can and expect Him to do the rest? And what could possibly be wrong with trying to find God within ourselves? Yet the travelers who follow these paths encounter bumps along the way—*barricades* might be a better word.

A friend of mine told me how guilty he felt when, as a youngster, he switched a sign on a street and watched as the motorists were misled. Signposts are important; if they are incorrectly labeled, the consequences can be disastrous.

Each of the three paths above share a common error. *They overestimate our ability and underestimate God's holiness.* They operate from a skewed perspective of ourselves. We see shades of goodness and badness, and as long as we compare ourselves to others, we can be quite confident that we are worthy of God's love and forgiveness.

We've all had that satisfied feeling that comes from doing our "good deed for the day." When we go the extra mile by taking care of our neighbor's children, giving some money to charity, or making an honest deal, we feel smug about our goodness. And when we pick up the newspaper and read about those who kill and steal, we feel pride at how different (and better) we really are. We might even think about how much better the world would be if everyone were just like us.

Our problem is that we are looking at ourselves through the wrong end of the telescope. We are actually much further from God than we can imagine. The better we understand God, the more convinced we will be that there is no recognizable common moral ground between us and Him. It turns out that we are like the boy who told his mother that he was eight feet tall, at least according to the yardstick *he* had made!

I can't speak for you, but my problem is that I'm not very good at climbing a ladder to God. No matter how hard I try, my basic nature remains unchanged. I can resolve to be better, and I might even improve, but I am fundamentally the same within. My problem is that after I climb the ladder a foot, I often fall back a yard. I mess up.

If we could grasp how holy God is, I am sure we would quickly agree that we have misjudged how far up the ladder we have come. Fact is, we even hide our true selves from ourselves, for, beneath it all, we are nasty sinners. I agree with Augustine, who said, "He who believes that God is holy will despair trying to appease him."

Later in this book I will explain why some people who take steps toward God might actually be taking steps away from Him. As we shall see, the harder we work to attain heaven, the less likely we are to make it. *Our good works give us a false sense of assurance because they mask our real need.*

Church rituals don't help much. The problem is that if I am accumulating grace through the sacraments, good works, and learning, I still don't know when I have enough. Even if I could take care of my past sins, tomorrow is another day.

Even the mystics had to admit that the more carefully they looked into their hearts, the more they realized that they could not love God unselfishly. The closer they got to God, the more clearly they saw their mixed motives. Yes, they loved God, but perhaps they did so out of fear of hell or out of a desire for self-fulfillment. Who can say that he loves God with pure, unselfish motives?

To really love God means we should hate sin. So these sincere souls tried to get themselves to hate what they knew they secretly loved! Try as they might, however, they could not uproot sin from within their hearts. Greed, lust, envy, self-will—those still lurked within the soul. Left unresolved was the question of how a holy God could meet them within their souls, which had not yet been purified. The more they contemplated their own hearts, the more sin they saw.

Whatever else may be said about the path of the mystics, it was simply not accessible to everyone. The common person who had to work long hours to earn a living had neither the time nor the opportunity to devote his life to mystical contemplation of God. And if those who did have such an opportunity confessed that they died without the assurance of salvation, the question was: Why bother?

When our oldest daughter was about ten years old, she talked us into buying a hamster. I felt sorry for that little animal, running on his wheel at all hours of the day. My response was to put a drop of oil on the wire axle so that I didn't have to hear the squeaking that came from his cage. If you are going to run on a treadmill, at least you should do so without disturbing others!

There is such a thing as a religious treadmill. When we are on that treadmill, there is no relief from the daily recognition that what we do is never enough, and there is no escape from the worry that, after we have expended all this energy, God just might put the bar a notch higher. We sympathize with the man who feared hearing the Lord tell Mother Teresa that she should have done more.

Some people have chosen to get off the treadmill altogether. They have left religion behind and seem to be content just doing the best they can, hoping that everything will turn out right. Many of them feel better because of it.

THE NARROW WAY THAT LEADS TO LIFE

C. S. Lewis said, "The safest road to hell is the gradual one; the gentle slope, soft underfoot, without sudden turnings, without milestones, without sign posts." Or, as we have learned, it is the attractive, well-traveled road with mislabeled signposts. You're convinced that this crowd of well-meaning people couldn't be wrong.

But if the lanes that look so right are really on the "broad way that leads to destruction," as Christ put it, how can we recognize the narrow way that leads to life? And how can we be sure that the path we chose is the right one? These questions will be answered more fully later on, but for now let's just think about what the narrow road would have to look like, given our predicament.

Since we will always fail at climbing the ladder to God, we need God Himself to come down the ladder and rescue us. We need God to initiate a plan that is so radical, so drastic, that it is independent of our own tainted efforts. We need a grand scheme that will overcome all of our shortcomings.

We need a way that doesn't appeal simply to those who have a bent toward religion; we need a help that isn't limited to those who were brought up in fine homes and have managed to stay out of trouble. The narrow way has to work for people regardless of their racial origin or their social and financial advantages (or disadvantages).

Realistically, this path should be open even to those who have failed "big time." You might know an alcoholic, a rapist, or even a murderer who is too morally weak, or too run-down, and has done too much damage to climb even the most user-friendly ladder to God. Some people, figuratively speaking, have fallen off the ladder completely. In fact, we all have.

Pastoring in downtown Chicago for so many years, I have come to realize that many people (more than we would like to admit) have done terrible things that they cannot change. I have met people who have destroyed other people's lives through abuse, drugs, and crimes. Some have broken marriages, angry children, and ruined careers. Some have well-hidden skeletons that torment them in moments of quietness and solitude.

These folks don't know where to begin in coping with their guilt and failure. They have done too much damage to be saved by good works. Nobody knows how much grace they would have to accumulate to become holy enough for God to receive them. For them, the paths that we have briefly explored simply will not do.

Finally, if there is a path that really does lead to God, we should know it. To put it differently, we should have the *assurance* that our relationship with God rests on a solid foundation.

What I long for, and what I think every person longs for, is the knowledge that my relationship with God is secure—permanently secure—not just for today, but for tomorrow and for all of eternity. And such knowledge should be available to all who sincerely desire it, no matter how messed up, no matter how great their sin or crimes.

Neither you nor I want to be among those who are banished from heaven because we were on the wrong path. We should welcome, rather than fear, an examination of our convictions. Christ taught that our eternal destiny is dependent on what we believe and on what we do with those beliefs.

So we must approach these questions with an open mind and a willingness to learn and have our convictions challenged. Someday many will have to admit ruefully that misplaced faith is worse than no faith at all.

The question is not whether a path looks good or even feels right. The question is: Is it God's way, or is it what I *think* is God's way?

Stay tuned.

CHAPTER TWO

WHY GRACE IS SO AMAZING

I was capable of anything. I had not the least fear of God before my eyes. . . . I not only sinned myself, but made it my study to tempt and seduce others."

Those words were written by John Newton, who was such a notorious sinner that he challenged his friends to think of some new sin he had not yet tried. He was a cruel slave trader who convinced himself that he was an atheist—and with God pushed out of his consciousness, anything was permissible.

But on March 10, 1748, while on board the vessel *Greyhound,* which was being ripped apart in a powerful storm, Newton remembered God. After hours of relentlessly pumping water from the ship, Newton, convinced that he was now to die, made a suggestion to the captain as to how the ship might be spared, and then he added, "If this will not do, the Lord have mercy on us!"

This was the first time he consciously spoke of his

need for the mercy of God. Now the question lodged in his mind: "What mercy can there be for *me?*"

He returned to his pump as the icy waves drenched him and his companion. Eventually, he and his mate stopped during a lull in the storm to tie themselves to the pump to be kept from being thrown into the sea. In his terror, verses from the Bible that his mother had taught him now raced through his mind. "Because I have called you, and ye refused; I stretched out my hand, and no one paid attention; . . . I will also laugh at your calamity; I will mock when your fear cometh" (Proverbs 1:24, 26 KJV). He had laughed at God; God was now laughing at him. The words kept coming back.

Every time the ship plunged and a watery mountain engulfed it, he was convinced that in a moment the vessel would be smashed to bits. Even yet, he wasn't convinced that the Christian religion was true. He had ridiculed the miracles of the New Testament for so long it was now difficult for him to believe.

The next day, when the storm subsided, the sailors went back to their responsibilities without giving thanks to God that their lives had been spared. Newton, however, found a New Testament that was on board and began to read it. He read chapter after chapter until he was convinced that Christ's death on the cross was for him. "It met my need exactly," he wrote later. "I needed someone to stand between me and a holy God who must punish my sins and blasphemies. I needed an Almighty Savior who would step in and take my sins away. . . . I saw that Christ took my punishment so that I might be pardoned."[1]

Twenty-seven days later, weak and starving, the crew reached land and were saved. Newton saw this as from the loving hand of God. Years later, he wrote what has become the most beloved hymn of all time:

Amazing Grace! how sweet the sound,
That saved a wretch like me!
I once was lost, but now am found,
Was blind, but now I see.

John Newton never again doubted God's grace—God's undeserved favor toward us. But many people who have never had an experience like his don't understand why grace is truly amazing. Or maybe they think that a sinner like Newton needed special grace, but they do not. They see grace as nice, helpful—even necessary—but not really *amazing.*

Here is something you can count on: *The better you believe yourself to be, the less grace you think you need.* The more self-confident you are, the more convinced you'll be that you could get by even if God were stingy with grace. Sure, you struggle with sin, but that's just a part of the human predicament. All you need is some help from God and a bit of personal determination. You can make yourself good enough for God to accept you. You just need to get desperate enough to clean up your act. If grace can help you—fine.

John Callaway, a well-known interviewer on the television program "Chicago Tonight," was asked about his religious faith. He said, "I'm struggling and I'm not winning that struggle. I'm living in the classic state of sin in that I think I'm separated from God. And my only saving grace is that I know it and I think I'll do something about it if I live long enough."[2] He added that he "just needed to get serious about it!"

Someday, when I get serious, I'll do something about it!

Even if Callaway had added, "With God's help I will do something when I get serious about it," he would not have understood grace. For him, apparently, grace is appreciated but not amazing. If he put his mind to it and did his part and if God graciously did His, together they could "pull it off."

God sees us quite differently. The New Testament paints a damning portrait of what our life is like without God's grace. Sure, hard work and discipline might change us, but they will not help one whit in bringing us closer to God. Our condition is far worse than we have ever dreamed. *Not until we know how bad off we are will we appreciate how good God is.* Grace then turns out to be amazing indeed.

LIFE WITHOUT GRACE

So, how bad off would we be without grace? In the New Testament, Paul likened his readers to corpses in a cemetery. "And you were dead in your trespasses and sins, in which you formerly walked according to the course of this world, according to the prince of the power of the air, of the spirit that is now working in the sons of disobedience" (Ephesians 2:1–2).

This does not mean that people who have never received God's special grace are always mean-spirited or do bad things. I have met people who are generous and kind who would not want to be called Christians; they may not believe in grace (as described here) at all. But even so, because they are sinners like the rest of us, the Bible teaches that they are "dead in trespasses and sins." There is a barrier between them and God that only grace can overcome.

So let's jump into our passage and try to understand this unflattering description. It is not a pretty picture, but I think you will agree that it rings true.

We Are the Walking Dead

We have all walked through cemeteries, with their rows of tombstones lining small paths. It is not just that the bodies lying beneath the surface are weak or sick; they are entirely helpless. If they are to come alive, they will need more than help—*they will need a miracle.*

Imagine the surprise if at a funeral the preacher or priest were to turn to the corpse and say, "If you just got serious about it, you could sit up, get out of that coffin, and walk!" Chances are, someone would call for help and people in uniforms would lead the minister away.

Spiritually speaking, we are dead toward God; and unless He gives us the miracle of life, we will stay dead. Of course, the people Paul is talking about in Ephesians are not dead physically, but spiritually. People who are "dead in trespasses and sins" might go to the symphony, watch a movie, or walk their dogs. Some might even be reading this book, proof that we can do many things while being alive in this world but dead toward God.

When our daughter Lisa was about four years old she said, "Mommy, my teddy bear knows that he isn't real!" We laughed, of course. When you stop to think about it, only a real teddy bear could know that he wasn't real.

Don't miss my point: Teddy bears can't know that they are real (or unreal), and they don't have the power to make themselves real. The same goes for people interred in cemeteries. A dead body can't make itself alive. Only God can return the spark of life to him. To continue the analogy: to expect people to rectify their relationship with God on their own is expecting the impossible. We cannot raise ourselves to life, even if we were to get serious about it.

Left to ourselves, we are disconnected from God just as surely as the plug of an electric lamp that has been pulled from the wall. And we cannot restore the current. Without Christ, we are "The Walking Dead."

Paul now explains in more detail what this means.

We Are Deceived by Satan

"The Devil made me do it!" was popularized by comedian Flip Wilson in the 1970s. Well, the Devil might have had something to do with it, but he didn't make us do it. We at least cooperated. But yes, we are deceived by Satan and his demons. Paul said that we walk "according to the prince of the power of the air, of the spirit that is now working in the sons of disobedience" (Ephesians 2:2). We are influenced by the one who is "the prince of this world" and who is continuously at work "among the sons of disobedience."

Christ taught that Satan has the ability to put thoughts into our minds that we think are our own! But he cannot do that unless we have already chosen to follow our own wisdom and our own desires. Whether the influence is direct or remote, great or small, an evil spirit with many helpers roams the earth trying to keep people from understanding the truth. That only adds to our deadness, the spiritual vacuum that fills the heart.

We make the problem worse through denial, by thinking we are something that we are not. Whether or not you agree with all that Luther wrote, you would have to agree that he had an interesting way of describing how deceived we really are without God's intervention. He wrote that the natural man was "bound, miserable, captive, sick and dead, but who by the operation of his lord, Satan, adds to his other miseries, blindness; so that he believes he is free, happy and at liberty, powerful, whole and alive."

Bad enough to be blind and dead, but imagine being blind and dead and thinking of yourself as seeing and alive!

We Are Depraved

Paul also said, "Among them we too all formerly lived in the lusts of our flesh, indulging the desires of the flesh and of the mind, and were by nature children of wrath, even as the rest" (Ephesians 2:3). We sin as naturally as a bird sprouts feathers. We are not sinners because we sin; we sin because we are sinners.

Sin is nothing more than putting myself first, serving myself as best I can. Sin is not first and foremost committing adultery, stealing, or even becoming involved in crime. The first commandment is that we love the Lord our God with all our mind, soul, and strength (see Matthew 22:37; Deuteronomy 6:5). It follows that when we love ourselves more than God, we are committing what might be the greatest sin.

Sin is choosing to do what I want without doing it in submission to God's will and plan. That is why I can be sinning even when I think I'm doing just fine on my own. In fact, I might be *especially* sinning at the moment I think I am doing just fine.

And though I think I am doing fine on my own, honesty compels me to realize that life without God has little real meaning. Feel the deadness of ordinary living expressed in these lines that a friend of mine found on a painting in one of his favorite cafes:

I have taken the pill
I have hoisted my skirts to my thighs
Dropped them to my ankles,
Rebelled at the University
Skied in Aspen
Lived with two men,
Married one.
Earned my keep
Kept my identity;
and frankly . . .
I'M LOST.

35

"If this is living, why do I feel so empty?" That is what many people ask themselves even though they might have all the friends money can buy. Even religious folks can experience spiritual "lostness." Anyone who looks for meaning in the wrong places will, if he is honest, confess that life seems trivial and without a grand purpose.

Perhaps you think that I have overstated the problem. But remember, I'm only helping us to understand what Paul wrote in the New Testament. By now it should be clear that we are in no condition to take care of our relationship with God. We need a heavy dose of grace. We need a big miracle, a breath of spiritual life from God. We need God to come to our rescue. Nothing less than a resurrection will do.

Grace has to be amazing or we are lost.

CHARACTERISTICS OF AMAZING GRACE

If the grace of God is to come to our rescue, it has to be powerful enough and merciful enough to meet us where we are and bring us into the presence of God. Paul continued, "But God, being rich in mercy, because of His great love with which He loved us, even when we were dead in our transgressions, made us alive together with Christ (by grace you have been saved), and raised us up with Him, and seated us with Him in the heavenly places, in Christ Jesus" (Ephesians 2:4–6).

God has entered the cemetery!

Grace Is Given Apart from Works

God surveyed the human race and concluded that He could not expect us to cooperate in reconciling ourselves to Him. Our fallenness permeated our entire being: our minds are tainted with sin, our souls are stained, and our wills are paralyzed. Good people or not, we are in deep trouble.

The apostle Paul would say to John Callaway, "Not only are you unable to do something about it, but your very act of trying to do something about it will complicate the problem! *Don't do anything about it until you have understood what God has done!*"

At last, I hope we are ready to define the word *grace*. Grace means God's undeserved favor. It is a gift that sets aside all human merit. It does not simply give us a hand, it gives us a resurrection. Grace is all one-sided.

Grace means that God takes the first step toward us. Yes, we do take a step because, unlike our daughter's teddy bear, we do have mind, emotions, and will. But our small step is simply a response to what God has already done. Grace means that God speaks a word, gives us spiritual life, and fits us to stand before Him. He descends the ladder we were trying to climb, scoops us up, and takes us all the way into His presence.

If God's rescue program had included our efforts, grace would be diminished and salvation would not be wholly the work of God. "But if it is by grace, it is no longer on the basis of works, otherwise grace is no longer grace" (Romans 11:6). Some things can exist together, but human works and the grace that brings salvation cannot.

To clear the field for His own activity, God eliminated every work of man—past, present, and future. His action had to be pure, uncontaminated by our own best efforts. He had to act alone. Our self-effort was put on a shelf labeled "Unsuitable for Use."

If God had found something truly good within us that He could have used, He would have been obligated to recognize it and reimburse us for it. If God had owed us salvation, the whole system of grace would have collapsed. But His analysis concluded that every good work we do is tainted. Even on our best days, our motives are mixed. It's not just our actions, it's also who we are: sinners with an infinite gap between ourselves and God.

Grace means that we deserve nothing and can do nothing. *God comes along and does what we cannot do.*

Grace Is Unaffected by the Degree of Our Sin

What about those who have really messed up in life? I am talking about those who are in a tangled mess, without much hope of recovering from their misdeeds. Just think of the person you believe has blown it more than any other. Can grace save him?

Let us suppose that you have two corpses. Is one more dead than another? Does one need a bigger miracle to be restored to life? Fact is, the good person who lives next to you and the criminal you read about in the newspaper are essentially in the same predicament—*both need the life that only God can give.*

Those of us who lived in Chicago in 1994 remember the hoopla surrounding the execution of John Wayne Gacy, who was convicted of killing thirty-three boys and hiding them in the crawl space under his house. The media wanted to make him out to be some kind of monster who was scarcely a member of the human race. What struck me, however, was how normal he looked. In fact, he looked a lot like someone I know.

Gacy did not have horns. He did not look as if devils were coming out of his body. What got lost in the news stories was that he was an ordinary man with whom all of us, as members of the human family, share a great deal. He was simply a human being who decided to follow perverted sexual desires wherever they might lead.

Gacy is a reminder of some words of wisdom I read somewhere: "Sin always takes you further than you intended to go, keeps you longer than you intended to stay, and costs you more than you intended to pay."

When he began his sinful lifestyle, he had no idea it would end where it did.

Aleksandr Solzhenitsyn, who had a better grasp of the human heart than most of us, realized that the evils of the Gulag do not belong to one race, country, or ideology. He wrote, "If only there were evil people somewhere insidiously committing evil deeds, and it were necessary only to separate them from the rest of us and destroy them. But the line dividing good and evil cuts through the heart of every human being."[3] Apart from grace, we are all on the same road. Some people just slide into the ditch and stay for a while. Others slide in, drag others in with them, and set up house.

Think of it this way. The Sears Tower in Chicago is much taller than the LaSalle National Bank. From our vantage point there is a great contrast between the height of these buildings. But let's suppose we changed the question and asked which one of them was closer to the constellation Orion, which is a few thousand light years away from the earth. Sure, the top of the Sears Tower is closer to this stellar constellation than the top of the bank, but does it really matter? *In the presence of thousands of trillions of miles, there is no appreciable difference in height between the two.*

Don't misinterpret what I'm saying. Of course it is better to be a decent citizen than to be John Wayne Gacy. Of course it is better to be honest than to be embezzling funds at work. From our point of view these distinctions are very significant, and they are also important to God. *But spiritually speaking, even the best of us is still an infinite distance from God.* If we forget this, it is because we have overestimated our goodness and underestimated God's holiness.

The good news is that God can save big sinners just as wonderfully as He can save lesser ones. God has declared that all of us are sinners and every mouth must be closed in His presence: "For there is no distinction; for all have sinned and fall short of the glory of God" (Romans 3:22–23). Some fall more short than others, but since the standard is God's glory, we all miss it. That's why we read that, from God's point of view, "there is no distinction."

Elsewhere Paul wrote, "But God has shut up all in disobedience that He might show mercy to all" (Romans 11:32). We are equal in our unbelief, equal in our sin, and therefore equal in our need for grace.

There is no evidence that John Wayne Gacy accepted God's grace as given in Christ, but if he had, he too would have died a forgiven man. Here is a message of hope: *The issue is never the greatness of the sin, but the willingness of the sinner to be saved.* And even this willingness, this desire to accept what Christ has done for us, is given to us by God's grace: "No one can come to Me, unless the Father who sent Me draws him; and I will raise him up on the last day" (John 6:44). Those are Christ's words, not mine!

Grace Is a Free Gift

If you have followed the logic so far, you know that grace has to be a free gift. Since it is independent of works and wholly of God, it must be given without strings attached. We now follow Paul's argument one step further. "For by grace you have been saved through faith; and that not of yourselves, it is the gift of God; not as a result of works, that no one should boast" (Ephesians 2:8–9).

When I was a child, my parents would have us listen to radio programs. There was one man who had a particular fascination for me because of his gruff voice and no-nonsense approach to teaching the Bible. But I also recall him saying something that did not make sense. At the end of the broadcast he said, "If you will send me five dollars, I will send you this new book, absolutely free!"

Even at the age of ten, I knew this was a contradiction. If he had really meant that the book was free, he would not only have sent it to anyone who requested it, he would have even paid the postage required to make the request. *That's what God does!*

Paul put it this way: "For the wages of sin is death, but the free gift of God is eternal life in Christ Jesus our Lord" (Romans 6:23). Yes, it has to be a gift—unearned and undeserved—and it is too expensive to repay.

Somewhere I read a story about a missionary who became a good friend of an Indian pearl diver. They had discussed salvation for many hours, but the Hindu could not believe that it could be a free gift. He believed that salvation could come by walking the nine hundred miles to Delhi on his knees. But the missionary said that salvation was so costly that Jesus had to buy it for us.

Before he left on his pilgrimage, the Indian gave the missionary the largest and most perfect pearl he had ever seen. The pearl diver explained that his own son had lost his life in getting this pearl from the bottom of the sea. The missionary thanked him, but then insisted that he pay for it. The Hindu was offended, saying that there was no price that could be paid for a pearl that had cost him his son.

Then and there the truth dawned: That is why Christians insist that no one can pay for salvation. It cost God the death of His only Son. To think we can pay for that is an insult indeed. *Grace is free to us but very costly to God.*

God is so rich, we surmise, that He would not have had to buy anything. But there is one thing that God has purchased, and that is His people. We were not redeemed with perishable things, such as silver or gold, "but with precious blood, as of a lamb unblemished and spotless, the blood of Christ" (1 Peter 1:19). To think that we could repay Him is an affront. It is a special insult when we attempt to repay Him with works He says He finds contemptible!

We will be indebted to God forever, but He has no expectation that we shall repay Him. If we think we can repay Him, we not only misunderstand the value of the gift, we also tarnish the word *grace*. God's favor toward us is undeserved, entirely a gift from Him to us. God doesn't expect to be paid back. He knows we can't. And we won't.

Grace Is Difficult to Accept

You'd think that everyone would be flocking to accept God's grace. Not so. There are reasons that the way to life is narrow and "few are those who find it" (Matthew 7:14).

Intuitively, we think that we have to have some part in our salvation, to do some work, some deed that will make us worthy of the gift. Some do this by working up a sorrow for sin. Such sorrow is proper and to be expected, but it is not the basis for God's loving favor toward us. Sorrow does not make us more worthy of God's grace. It might lead us to cast ourselves upon His grace, but it will never make us more "presentable."

Someone said to me, "When I become older, I will come to God because then I will be less prone to failure." Whenever you meet a person who talks like that, you know that he has not yet understood grace. He is still thinking that he cannot come to God just as he is.

Many years ago I counseled a husband and wife who had come to church because their marriage was falling apart. I got the impression that the wife had dragged her husband to the meeting. I could tell that he wanted to be there about as much as a counterfeit coin wants to be seen on an offering plate.

They had belonged to a wife-swapping club, and the wife had recently come to understand the grace of God. She received the miracle of life that Christ offers, and it changed her. Now she wanted to get her husband to repent and experience the same miracle.

When I spoke to him, he said, "I would be lying to you if I told you that I won't continue in the club—I'm hooked." Of course he admitted that what he was doing was both sinful and destructive, but he felt that the temptation was too great. He could not change. He felt locked into his lifestyle.

I asked if he would be willing to admit his sinfulness and helplessness, to confess that he could not change himself. I urged him also to acknowledge that only Christ could forgive his sin and give him the miracle of eternal life. I explained that he didn't just need God's help; he even needed more than God's forgiveness. He needed God's power from start to finish.

For the first time in his life, he humbled himself to receive the grace of God, to accept Christ as having died in his stead as his sin-bearer. For days I wondered about him, hoping that the gospel would prove powerful in his life. To my relief, he made an appointment with me a few weeks later to say that he had left the club and was applying to a Bible school to train for Christian ministry.

He learned two things. First, *grace is free to helpless sinners who know how bad off they really are.* And second, *once the gift of grace is received no one can ever really be the same again.* We come to God as we are, but He does not leave us as He found us. You can come as a homosexual; you can come as an alcoholic; you can come as an adulterer; but you come to the only One who can give you the gift of grace.

There are two kinds of people who shy away from God's grace. We ourselves have probably felt torn between both ends of the spectrum.

First, those who are awash with guilt find grace difficult to accept. They think, *If you really knew ... if you knew what was in my past ... if you knew my secret life ... you would know that I'm too great a sinner to accept God's grace.* They are convinced that God is so mad at them there is no hope. They compare themselves to others and revise their estimation of themselves downward.

Second, the religious types, the Goody Two-shoes who think they have never done a very bad thing, find it difficult to accept God's grace. I remember a person saying that the worst thing he ever did in his whole life was to hit a golf ball through a window. Whew!

The folks who pay their bills, volunteer to work in the hospital, and raise good families find it difficult to accept God's grace because they don't think they need it. They know a dozen people who are worse than they. They look deeply into their hearts and realize that they could never do what John Wayne Gacy did. They see themselves as better than a whole host of other people. As one man told me, "I have just as good a shot at heaven as anyone else!"

These folks are offended when they are told that, in themselves, they are as far from God as John Wayne Gacy. They bristle at the suggestion that the distance between themselves and God is infinite. They compare themselves to someone who is worse than they and revise their estimation of themselves upward.

That explains why Christ said that the prostitutes will enter the kingdom of heaven ahead of the religious types. Those who are in despair are more likely to see their need of God's grace than those who are self-assured. *Those who know they need a miracle are more likely to receive grace than those who think they just need God's help.*

Grace Can Be Received

Sometimes preachers who should know better speak of receiving God's grace as if we were expected to make a bargain with Him. I have a friend (bless him!) who in his witness for Christ used to tell people to "pledge their allegiance to Jesus Christ." An evangelist gave an invitation and told the people coming forward that they were making a "promise to follow Christ." I shake my head in dismay!

The potential convert is thinking, *If I have to pledge my allegiance to Jesus Christ or promise to follow Him, what will happen if I make such a decision and then break my promise the next day?* Certainly, accepting God's grace will result in a change of lifestyle. But we cannot expect the dead to walk until they are raised and the blind to see until they are healed. Sinners who have never been reconciled to God do not have the power to change their lifestyles, even if they were to get "really serious" about it.

To the person who says, "I want to do something about my broken relationship with God," grace says, "If you really understood the issues you wouldn't talk that way. God *did* something about your broken relationship with Him, and the only thing you can do is to humble yourself and accept it!"

Let me be clear. When you come to Christ, you do not come to *give,* you come to *receive.* You do not come to *try your best,* you come to *trust.* You do not come just to be *helped,* but to be *rescued.* You do not come to be *made better* (although that does happen), you come to be *made alive!*

Augustus Toplady had it right:

Nothing in my hands I bring,
Simply to Thy cross I cling;
Naked, come to Thee for dress,
Helpless, look to Thee for grace;
Foul, I to the fountain fly;
Wash me, Savior, or I die!

You do not come to Christ to make a promise; you come to depend on His promise. It is the faithfulness of God and not your own that gives the gift of grace.

TWO MEN, TWO BELIEFS, TWO DESTINIES

Christ told a story about two men who both believed in grace. Yet interestingly, only one experienced the miracle of God's acceptance. The other, good man though he was, was rejected.

When the religious Pharisee went into the temple, he prayed thus: "God, I thank Thee that I am not like other people: swindlers, unjust, adulterers, or even like this tax-gatherer. I fast twice a week; I pay tithes of all that I get" (Luke 18:11–12).

If we think he was bragging, let's remember that he believed in grace. He *thanked God* that he was not like other men; He knew that his good works were done because of God's goodness, and he admitted it. I can hear him saying, "But for the grace of God, there go I." If he was better than others, God deserved the credit.

In contrast, the tax-gatherer who was standing next to him was so overwhelmed by his sin that he would not even lift his face to heaven but smote his breast and said, "God, be merciful to me, the sinner!" (verse 13).

Christ added, "I tell you, this man went down to his house justified rather than the other; for every one who exalts himself shall be humbled, but he who humbles himself shall be exalted" (verse 14).

Yes, both men believed in God's grace. The self-righteous Pharisee thought that God's grace was only needed to do good deeds. God's grace, he thought, helps us do better.

The tax-gatherer saw God's grace differently. He knew that if he were to be saved, it would take a miracle that only God could do. He didn't need just a little help; he needed the gift of forgiveness, the gift of reconciliation. Only God could do what needed to be done.

The Pharisee said, "God, if You help me, I'll do better and save myself!"

The tax-gatherer said, "God, You save me, or I'll damn myself!"

Was it difficult for this sinner—this tax-gatherer—to receive grace? Depends. On the one hand, no, for he was relieved to discover that there was grace for the needy. But on the other hand, the grace of God was very difficult to accept. The crushing experience of having to admit total helplessness apart from God's grace is not easy for any man. *And that is why the way to life is narrow and few there be that find it.*

Suppose you were standing at the door of the temple, and, as the Pharisee brushed by, you told him that he was spiritually lost. He would have been insulted. He would have admitted that he was a sinner but, with a shrug, would have reminded you that he was doing something about it and could do more if he got more serious! Grace was helpful and even necessary, but not amazing.

And that, at the end of the day, is the difference between those who are saved and those who are lost. Those who think they can contribute to their salvation think that God's grace is wonderful; but only the humble, who see themselves as God does, believe it is amazing indeed. *The difference is between those who know that God has to do it all and those who think that they can help Him out.*

The fourth stanza of the well-known and loved hymn "Amazing Grace" captures the wondrous nature of grace. Neither our life on earth nor our stay in heaven will exhaust our wonder.

> *When we've been there ten thousand years,*
> *Bright shining as the sun,*
> *We've no less days to sing God's praise*
> *Than when we first begun.*

Yes, grace is all one-sided. We bring nothing to the table, except our sins. God brings everything we need to lift us into His presence.

Amazing indeed!

NOTES

1. John Newton, *Out of the Depths* (reprint; Chicago: Moody Press, Moody Literature Ministry, n.d.), 81–82.
2. John Calloway, *Chicago Tribune,* 22 April 1994.
3. Aleksandr Solzhenitsyn, *Christianity Today,* 7 February 1994.

CHAPTER THREE

THE GIFT WE CAN'T DO WITHOUT

I'm sure you've met someone who enjoys making a nuisance of himself!

A friend of mine attended the prestigious annual Christian Booksellers Convention. Tape recorder in hand, he went about asking the participants a pesky question. These were the folks who wrote books about Christian living and the latest trends in theology, and every one of them should have known the answer to my friend's query, but most didn't.

Specifically, what he asked was, "Do you believe that we have to be perfect to enter into heaven?" A few knew the answer, but most stumbled through their reply, saying, with a shrug, something like, "No, we don't have to be perfect. Thanks to God's mercy, He doesn't require this of us or we wouldn't make it!"

God, they believed, is lenient, and we have reason to assume that He will allow us as sinners into His presence. In fact, He is so gracious that, thanks to Christ, the standards have been lowered. "Christians," they said, "are not perfect, just forgiven!" With a bit of His help, a dose of His forgiveness, and a tad of His grace, we can make it.

How would you have answered that question? Perhaps you have never thought of it before, so I'll answer it for you. *Christianity, both Catholic and Protestant, has always taught that we have to be as perfect as God to stand in His presence.* Nothing less will do. So let me be as clear as possible. If you are not as perfect as God, don't even think you will ever be admitted into the heavenly realms! Give up your dreams.

The answer every delegate should have given was "Of course I have to be as perfect as God if I expect to stand before Him and be welcomed and received into His presence!" Come to think of it, this is not only the teaching of the Bible, but it also makes good sense. How could an infinitely pure and holy God who passionately hates sin have fellowship with people who are still regarded as sinners?

God's grace does not mean that the standard has been lowered. It doesn't mean that God can overlook our sin. Yes, God's grace means that we can be forgiven, but it means a lot more than that. But I'm ahead of the story.

Now, if we have to be as perfect as God to enter into heaven (and we do), then we have an obvious problem. In the last chapter I described as best I could how bad off we really are when left to ourselves. We are sinners by nature and sinners by choice. Some of us have done some wretched things. I have never yet met anyone who believes that he or she is as perfect as God.

So the question is this: How can we become as perfect as the Almighty Himself? That's a tall order, and it is also the subject of this chapter.

ONE MAN'S STRUGGLE
TO ACHIEVE PERFECTION

I have some Roman Catholic friends who think that Martin Luther was a turncoat, a deranged man who was angry at the church of his time for petty, personal reasons. Well, I'm not going to defend everything Luther did or wrote. Luther said and did some foolish things. Sometimes he was coarse, often angry.

But whether you are Catholic or Protestant, you have to appreciate his personal struggle. I myself am not a Lutheran, but Luther's experience has something to say to us all. Before we dismiss him out of hand, we must try to push back the curtain and understand the war within his soul.

Luther was troubled by what is known in German as *Anfechtungen,* a recurring despair of the soul. He was plagued by a keen sense of his own sin. Try as he might, he could not find peace.

He was taught a truth, apparently lost to our generation, that we have to be as perfect as God to enter heaven. But the path to becoming perfect, or holy, was tortuous and fraught with obstacles. Those who were serious about their faith would avail themselves of the means of grace offered by the church, and Luther did this to the best of his ability.

The church held out to people the possibility of embarking on the journey toward holiness. Those few who attained this perfection were canonized as saints, apparently qualified to enter heaven immediately at death. Those who did not attain this high degree of sainthood went to purgatory for as long as was needed until they were purged of their sins. Eventually, they, too, would qualify for the perfections of heaven, although no one knew when.

Luther longed for the assurance that he would meet whatever standard God required. He fasted so long that his friends feared for his health. He often wore rough clothing and slept in his cold cell without blankets to "put to death" the desires of the flesh. But no matter what he did, it never seemed to be enough.

Second, he took advantage of the sacraments of the church. Confession was of some comfort to him. To remind himself of his failures, he would begin by reciting the seven deadly sins and the Ten Commandments. Sometimes he confessed his sins for up to six hours and then later would go to his confessor, Staupitz, because he remembered a sin he had overlooked. One day Staupitz was so exasperated he said, "If you expect Christ to forgive you, come in with something to forgive—parricide, blasphemy, adultery—instead of these peccadilloes!"

Some have suggested that Luther was mentally imbalanced because he was so concerned about trifles. But he was perhaps the only sane man in the monastery. He knew that it mattered not whether the sin was big or little, but whether it had been forgiven. Even the smallest sin was enough to keep one from heaven forever. He knew that one blemish would bar us from the unimaginable majesty of God.

In his quest for perfection, Luther reached an impasse. He had been taught that if sin were to be forgiven, it had to be confessed. His problem was (1) that he could not be sure that he could remember all of his sins; (2) that he might have done some things he didn't realize were sins, so they would remain unconfessed; and (3) that even if he remembered and confessed all of his sins, tomorrow was another day, and the process had to begin all over again.

To make matters worse, he realized that his whole nature was corrupt. He was not a sinner because he sinned.

Rather—and this was much more ominous—he sinned because he was at root a sinner. There were not only deeds that had to be confessed but thoughts too. The longer he lived, the more there would be of them. More penance, more confessions, more prayers.

Somewhere I read this bit of advice: "When you are in a hole, the first rule is to stop digging!" Well, Luther was in a hole, and he kept digging—trying to get out of the swamp of sin that lay in his heart. But he could not make himself free, even though he called on God for help. In desperation, he went beyond what the church had prescribed. Yet he was not sure that he had satisfied God on so much as a single point. To Luther, being promised eternal life was like a blind man's being promised a million dollars if only he opened his eyes to see. The promise was wonderful, but the conditions were impossible.

In 1511, Luther was assigned to teach philosophy at the fledgling university in Wittenberg, which had been founded by the Elector Frederick. Luther enjoyed his work, but his conscience could not be silenced. One day when Staupitz visited him, he suggested that Luther should begin to teach the Bible in hopes of finding some solace for his soul.

And so it was that in 1513 Luther began lecturing on the Psalms and came to the first verse of Psalm 22: "My God, my God, why hast thou forsaken me?" He knew that these were the words Christ quoted on the cross. Christ, too, had *Anfechtungen,* for His soul was in despair. Luther realized that this was because Christ had taken our sin upon Himself.

In his study of the book of Romans, he soon came to these words: "For I am not ashamed of the gospel, for it is the power of God for salvation to every one who believes, to the Jew first and also to the Greek. For in it the righteousness of God is revealed from faith to faith; as it

is written, 'But the righteous man shall live by faith'"
(Romans 1:16–17). Luther struggled with the expression
"the righteousness of God," which he correctly understood as an attribute that stands over us and judges us
and finds us to be unworthy. It is the righteousness of
God that exposes our puny righteousness and makes us
look so deficient.

"Sometimes Christ seems to me nothing more than an
angry judge who comes to me with a sword in His hand,"
Luther remarked. The revelation of the righteousness of
God, he believed, was bad news, not good news. Since
we are punished for falling short of God's righteousness,
it was not exactly comforting to know more about how
holy God is! It makes us only the more convinced that we
are sinners. We can increase our performance, but God's
standard is far beyond us. The thought of trying harder
sent Luther further into depression.

He described his struggle. "My situation was that, although an impeccable monk, I stood before God as a
sinner troubled in conscience, and I had no confidence
that my merit would assuage him. Therefore I did not
love a just and angry God, but rather hated and mur-
mured against him." Strong words, but the man was
desperate.

Fortunately, he continued to study the next chapters in
Romans, and the light dawned. He discovered that there
is also a righteousness *from* God, which is given as a gift
to sinners. For us, this is an alien righteousness because
it is not a part of our nature, nor is it something that is
fused into us. It remains external to us. *It is a righteousness that God credits to sinners who believe in Christ.*

Listen to Paul: "But now apart from the Law the righteousness of God has been manifested, being witnessed by
the Law and the Prophets, even the righteousness of God
through faith in Jesus Christ for all those who believe; for

there is no distinction; for all have sinned and fall short of the glory of God" (Romans 3:21–23). There is a *gift* of righteousness from God that comes apart from works.

We are thankful, for Luther and for us, that God can give us what we can never achieve. "For we maintain," Paul wrote, "that a man is justified by faith apart from works of the Law" (3:28). There is a sharp distinction between the righteousness of God and the righteousness of man. God's righteousness is not simply man's righteousness lifted to a higher level; no, it is of an entirely different sort. Just as a billion bananas added together will never make an orange, so all the human righteousness performed since Adam, added together, could never change God's attitude toward a single sinner. There is an infinite chasm between God's righteousness and ours.

Christ's righteousness is the exact kind of righteousness God requires—obviously so, for it is His very own! With it, a man can stand before God.

The question then becomes, "What must we do to receive this righteousness, this right standing with God?" The answer is that this righteousness is a gift that has to be received by faith. It is given to those who turn away from their own efforts and trust Christ to receive from Him something they do not have. This righteousness, once received, carries a man safely all the way to heaven.

Little wonder Luther said that embracing this discovery caused him to be "reborn and enter into the gates of paradise." Christ did for him what his works could never do!

This is known as "justification by faith," which can be defined as *God's decision to declare us to be as righteous as He Himself is.* The penalty for our sin has been paid by Christ, who met requirements that were infinitely beyond us.

In California, I am told, a man pleaded guilty to a traffic violation. The judge read out the sentence, then left the bench and paid the fine he had assessed. That is what God did. We owed Him what we could not pay; Christ, the second person of the Trinity, paid our debt for us. God's requirements were legally met. Those who believe have their debt canceled.

This, then, is *justification by grace alone, through faith alone, because of Christ alone.* Justification by faith changes the way God sees us, not the way we see ourselves. It refers to the work of God outside of us, namely, the gift of righteousness we receive.

Paul goes out of his way to show that even the Old Testament patriarch Abraham was justified by faith, for he *believed God* and it was "reckoned to him as righteousness" (Romans 4:3). That means simply that the righteousness of God was legally credited to his account. No one past or present can be saved without it.

In another passage, Paul explained, "He made Him who knew no sin to be sin on our behalf, that we might become the righteousness of God in Him" (2 Corinthians 5:21). So there are two incredible transactions that happened when Jesus died on the cross. *Christ was regarded as a sinner when He bore our sin; we are regarded as saints when we receive His righteousness.*

Just as Christ did not personally commit any sin, and yet we read, "He was made sin for us," so, though we personally are not righteous, we nevertheless are accounted as such. We have "become the righteousness of God." We are declared to be as perfect as God. In His presence God does not see us standing alone. He sees only His Son standing alone, and we are "in Him." And when sin has been laid on the Substitute, it can never be laid back on the sinner.

The cross was not simply an expression of mercy. It was also a display of justice. To put it clearly, Christ became legally guilty of breaking every one of the Ten

Commandments. He became legally guilty of genocide, sexual perversions, and hatred. Those sins were never a part of His nature or a part of His practice. They were alien sins borne by Him for us. Our debts were transferred to His account.

The result is exactly what we need. With God's righteousness ours, the legal logjam was broken. The dilemma of how a holy God could have fellowship with fallen humanity was solved. This explains why the New Testament can say that we are Christ's brothers: we are "heirs of God and fellow heirs with Christ" (Romans 8:17).

Sometimes justification has been defined as "just as if I'd never sinned." But that is only half the story. It is not just that our slate is clean, wonderful though that is. It is also that God looks at us as if we have lived lives of perfect obedience. He sees us as being loving, submissive, pure. *He sees us as having done everything Christ has done.*

If you have been reading this book for a while, this might be the place to put it down, get on your knees, and thank God for His incredible generosity. Or, if you have never received this gift of righteousness, receive it right now, by faith. This is grace indeed.

And the good news gets even better when we begin to contemplate the characteristics of this gift of perfect righteousness.

CHARACTERISTICS OF THIS RIGHTEOUSNESS

No wonder Paul kept returning to the theme of the righteousness of God! To the church in Philippi, he wrote that his goal was to be "found in Him, not having a righteousness of my own derived from the Law, but that which is through faith in Christ, the righteousness which comes from God on the basis of faith" (Philippians 3:9).

No doctrine is more central to our faith; none is as liberating; none is more necessary.

This Righteousness Is a Gift

Obviously the righteousness of God would have to be a gift, for we neither have it nor deserve it. To quote Paul once more, we are "justified as a gift by His grace through the redemption which is in Christ Jesus" (Romans 3:24).

Luther described this righteousness as "passive righteousness," for we receive it without doing anything. When we see the law, we see our sinfulness. All that we can think of are the sins we have committed and the things we should have done. Satan will take advantage of those weaknesses, and our consciences will be troubled, terrified, and confused.

Luther continues, saying that just as the earth does not produce rain but must simply receive it as a gift from above, so we can do nothing but receive this gift of righteousness. The soil cannot brag, for it neither deserved nor caused the refreshment. The parched ground is passive. It simply receives blessings by the mercy of God.

Once the earth has been watered, it can bear fruit, just as we will bear fruit for God after we have been granted the righteousness by faith. As for the terrors of the law—those penalties for sin we know we deserve—we need no longer fear, for Christ covers us. He is our refuge and strength.

While counseling a man who believed he had committed too many evils to be accepted by God, I asked him to visualize his life as a road on which he had carved some deep ruts, some leading right into the ditch. There were sins (or crimes) done against others that could never be rectified. All roads have their messes, but his was particularly ugly.

Then I asked him to visualize a blanket of two feet of snow covering the trail he had left behind. No matter how much the mud and gravel of the trail have been disturbed, no matter how deep the ruts or untidy the ditch, the snow covers it all. His past could be similarly covered, just as much as the path followed by the person next to him who all his life has tried his best to stay on the road. "'Come now, and let us reason together,' says the Lord, 'though your sins are as scarlet, they will be as white as snow; though they are red like crimson, they will be like wool'" (Isaiah 1:18).

Again I have to stress that I'm not saying that it doesn't matter what we do in life because God just comes along and covers our mess. Obviously, it is better to live a decent life than to live a destructive one. The lives we live have repercussions that continue after we have been justified. But as I emphasized in the last chapter, my point is that when it comes to the righteousness of God, the "good" person and the criminal must both receive it as a gift—a gift that covers the sins of the past, no matter how great or small.

God does not have to do anything "extra" to save hard-boiled, great, cruel sinners. Nor does He have an easier time saving decent, respectable sinners. The gift of righteousness—the snow, if you please—is able to cover a trail that is unusually ugly as well as one that has been carefully traveled. In either case, God has to do everything that needs to be done.

The grace of justification stands entirely alone. One writer, describing the relative differences between people, put it this way, "Grace . . . is not less than it would be had they sinned less. It is not more than it would be had they sinned more. It is wholly unrelated to every question of human merit." So it is. The righteousness of God is a gift given to all who truly believe.

Don't forget that God does not owe us this gift of righteousness. Fact is, if He gave it to us because He was obligated to, it wouldn't really be a gift. If we even partially deserved it, we could say that God was under some kind of obligation to give it to us. Grace means that what we received is completely undeserved.

That is why all the credit for our salvation goes to God alone. There is no room for boasting, no opportunity to say that we deserved it or helped Him with it. All we did was receive it by faith, which itself is not a work but a special gift of God.

I want the most wicked person reading this (I'll let you be the judge!) to know that Christ came to justify wicked people. We do not have to merit the merit of Christ!

This Righteousness Is Unchangeable

Obviously, everyone who receives this gift receives the same kind of righteousness. Whether it was the apostle Paul, who wrote much of the New Testament; or Billy Graham, who has preached to millions; or Bernard of Clairvaux, who inspired generations—these folks all received the same righteousness we do. Even ordinary people like us have the same acceptance before God, the same spiritual privileges.

Because I am a minister, I am usually asked to pray at church functions, whether they be picnics, banquets, or weddings. Somewhere, people have picked up the notion that pastors are closer to God and have a better chance of having their prayers answered. But anyone can pray just as effectively; anyone has the same friendship with God, providing that he or she has been made perfect through receiving this special gift.

This doctrine of equality is called "the priesthood of the believer." Every believer has the privileges of sonship. Every believer has the same attention, the same opportunity to serve God.

Nothing can ever be added to God's righteousness to make it better; nothing can be taken from it to lessen its value. A million years from now, it will still be as pristine as it was the day Jesus gave His life that we might have it. It is as unchangeable as God.

You don't have to know how to pronounce the name Nicolaus Zinzendorf to be blessed by these lines that he wrote:

> *Jesus, Thy blood and righteousness*
> *My beauty art, my glorious dress;*
> *'Midst flaming worlds, in these arrayed,*
> *With joy shall I lift up my head.*

This Righteousness Is Permanent

We learned that when Martin Luther was confessing his sins in a monastery, he always feared that he might have forgotten some or simply didn't recognize others. What frustrated him was the realization that even if he could somehow settle his accounts with God today, tomorrow the process would have to begin again. He always felt off balance in his relationship with God. To confess his sins was like trying to mop up the floor with the faucet running.

What Luther needed was a divine act that would settle his relationship with God once and for all. He needed the assurance that despite the sins that he would commit tomorrow, his future with God was taken care of.

Similarly, there are people today who confess their sins but still have no assurance that they have satisfied God's requirements. And with good reason. They, like Luther, must discover that confession is not the same as accepting the righteousness of God for all of our sins. We are not saved by confessing, but by believing.

Confession is to be practiced by those who are *already* God's children through justification by faith. Confession keeps us in fellowship with God. But before we do that, we need to have our legal relationship with God taken care of. God needs to do a lasting act that will make us His children forever.

Confession is not the starting point for sinners, but follows once salvation has been received. Confession keeps me in agreement with God, but I have to belong to Him before it has meaning. The good news of justification is that the righteousness of God covers us from now through eternity. Two thousand years ago, sins that we would one day commit were laid upon Christ. To trust Him is to receive the completed gift of righteousness that will settle our legal obligations with God forever.

Justification is not a long, tortuous process with an uncertain ending. Justification is trusting Christ to meet the continual demands of God in our behalf. Twenty-four hours a day God demands perfection; twenty-four hours a day Christ is my righteousness before God. He will be there for me tomorrow and the day after. As we shall see in a future chapter, He is committed to bring us all the way home.

Notice how clearly the author of Hebrews teaches the completeness of Christ's sacrifice and the finality of our justification before God. "By this will we have been sanctified through the offering of the body of Jesus Christ once for all. . . . For by one offering He has perfected for all time those who are sanctified" (Hebrews 10:10, 14). There was but *one* offering of Christ, and those who trust in it are "perfected for all time." We are not justified bit by bit as we perform religious duties. We are justified in *one* complete act.

Obviously, if justification took care of only our past sins, our future relationship with God would be in constant jeopardy. Tomorrow would be another day, with its temptations and sins, and I could commit a big sin and die. If all of my confessions and good deeds were not up-to-date, I would lose what I had yesterday. I'm glad that's not what the Bible teaches.

I have known a number of Christians who committed suicide. One woman showed me her husband's suicide note, which said that he could not "bear the thought of further suffering." Though he was a committed Christian, had led Bible studies, and brought others to faith in Christ, he decided to end his pain.

A girl felt so unloved that she reasoned that she was doing her family a favor when she took sleeping pills. Some people think that all who commit suicide go to hell, because they have committed a sin for which they cannot ask forgiveness. But the good news is that those who have had the righteousness of God credited to them will be saved, even if they should end in such failure. Suicide is a serious sin (murder), but thanks be, Christ died even for such sinners.

Once Luther grasped the fact that Christ's death paid every whit of the righteousness he owed God, he dropped the teaching of purgatory, which, interestingly, is not found in the Bible. The idea that we have to add our agony to the work of Christ, or that we still have to be further purified, diminishes Christ's work for us. Christ paid our debt *in full*. When we die, there is no intermediate stop.

Augustine, well aware of his own sin, cried out, "O, God, demand what you will, but supply what you demand!" And when God supplies what He demands, we can be sure that those demands have been fully met. The hymn writer Elvina Hall had it right:

Jesus paid it all,
All to Him I owe;
Sin had left a crimson stain,
He washed it white as snow.

Just think: The works of Christ belong to us just as much as if we personally performed them! We owe God no righteousness, for we are accepted on Christ's merit.

This Righteousness Guarantees God's Unconditional Love

In most American homes children get the impression that their parents' love for them is conditional, that is, dependent on the child's performance. I don't know how many times I've heard someone tell me, "If I got a B my dad would chide me for not getting an A. If I got an A, he wondered why it wasn't an A+." Inevitably, the child grew up believing he would be loved only if he would perform.

Consider: Because we are accepted in Christ, it would be heresy to say that God would love us more if only we were better. God loves us through Christ and, therefore, He loves us just as much as He loves Christ.

If you think I have overstated the case, ponder these words in Christ's prayer to His Father: "And the glory which Thou hast given Me I have given to them; that they may be one, just as We are one; I in them, and Thou in Me, that they may be perfected in unity, that the world may know that Thou didst send Me, and didst love them, even as Thou didst love Me" (John 17:22–23).

God loves Christ. Therefore He also loves us, for we are seen as being "in Christ," clothed with His perfections. Christ does not have some sort of righteousness we lack, for He shares His with us.

William Cowper, whose story will be told later in this book, wrote:

> *How Thou canst think so well of me*
> *And be the God thou art*
> *Is darkness to my intellect*
> *But sunshine to my heart.*

Of course, once we are God's children we can either please God or displease Him by the way we live. We must distinguish between our legal acceptance in Christ (our *position*) and our *practice* in daily living. Now that we know that we are loved, we will seek to love God. "We love, because He first loved us" (1 John 4:19).

This Righteousness Unites Us with Christ

We all saw the Rodney King beating on videotape that was widely used by the media to put the spotlight on police brutality. Every time King tried to stand up he was beaten down. About all that he could do was crawl, and even that was met with resistance.

That is a picture of the conflict within our souls. Being "saved" (that's a word often used in the Bible to describe those who are justified) does not mean that we are exempt from trials, temptations, and sins. Often when we want to stand, we find ourselves tripped up or beaten down.

But we *can* stand. We are united with Christ by faith, so we can stand in His strength. We are not overcome by pressures or even our own failures. We rejoice that today Christ is to us everything we need: "But by His doing you are in Christ Jesus, who became to us wisdom from God, and righteousness and sanctification, and redemption" (1 Corinthians 1:30).

The expression "in Christ Jesus" occurs more than one hundred times in the writings of Paul. Sometimes Bible teachers have called our union with Christ positional truth; that is, it refers only to our legal standing with God. Correct though this is, being "in Christ" is *reality;* it does not get any more real than this! This new relationship not only affects the way we see ourselves but becomes the basis for our encouragement and strength.

A woman, spiritually defeated because of a failed marriage and having little hope for a happy future, wrote to me that she had "given up on trying to ever please God." I replied that she need not feel helpless despite her setbacks, for, if she trusted Christ, He had already pleased God for her! Of course, she should try to please God in her daily living, but her efforts could never be the basis for her acceptance with God. The only sure basis for her relationship with God would always be Christ, not herself.

When the voice of conscience tells us that we are unworthy, when we are overcome by the consequences of our actions, believing that we can never forgive ourselves, we can confidently affirm, "Today God accepts me just as He accepts Christ. Today Christ is my representative, and He is standing in on my behalf."

Being "in Christ" gives us the assurance that we are heard in prayer. Calvin wrote, "It is a plain matter, that we cannot come boldly before the tribunal of God, unless we are certainly persuaded that He is our Father; and this cannot be without our being regarded as righteous in His sight."

THE TALE OF TWO BOOKS

In a discussion, a friend said to me, "There are so many different religions in the world, how can I possibly know which one is right?" I replied by saying that I would simplify matters for him. I would show that there are only two religions in the world.

I took a sheet of paper, drew a line down the middle, and above one column wrote, "All religions that teach we help save ourselves." Above the other column I wrote, "All religions that teach that God has done everything required to save us."

In a moment it became obvious that all the religions of the world belonged on the left side of the page. Christianity alone belonged on the right side.

The chasm between these two views is infinite and unbridgeable. The distance is as great as between heaven and hell, God and Satan, hope and hopelessness.

Recently I presided at the memorial service of a young man named Roger, who had died of AIDS. Though he had accepted Christ as his sin-bearer, and thus had the righteousness of God credited to his account, he still struggled with homosexuality until he was infected with HIV. Thereafter, he broke with his past behavior and lived a life of devotion to Christ. In the hospital, he was a witness to Christ's grace, especially to those who struggled with the same lifestyle and the same disease.

In his final days, it would have been easy for Roger to focus on his past behavior, the messy ruts he had made along the path of life. But he didn't. He focused on his acceptance in Christ, that gift of perfect righteousness which gave him the assurance that he would be welcomed into heaven. I am convinced that at death he entered heaven as perfect as God.

Imagine a book entitled *The Life and Times of Jesus Christ*. It contains all the perfections of Christ: the works He did, His holy obedience, His purity, His right motives. A beautiful book indeed.

Then imagine another book, *The Life and Times of Roger*. It contains all of his sins, immorality, broken promises, and betrayal of friends. It would contain sinful thoughts, mixed motives, and acts of disobedience.

Finally, imagine Christ taking both books and stripping them of their covers. Then He takes the contents of His own book and slips it between the covers of Roger's book. We pick up the book to examine it. The title reads, *The Life and Times of Roger.* We open the book and turn the pages and find no sins listed. All that we see is a long list of perfections, obedience, moral purity, and perfect love. The book is so beautiful that even God adores it.

This exchange is known as justification. It is crediting the loveliness of Christ to those who are woefully imperfect. *Of course we have to be perfect to enter into heaven, and, thanks to Christ, we are!*

> *The terrors of law and of God*
> *With me can have nothing to do*
> *My Savior's obedience and blood*
> *Hide all of my sins from view*
> *My name on the palm of His hands*
> *Eternity cannot erase*
> *Forever there it remains*
> *In marks of indelible grace!*

And the story is not yet over.

$\mathcal{T}$HE MIRACLE
WE NEED

Religion can be boring.

You don't have to do any research to prove the point. Just compare the crowd at church with the crowds that attend baseball or football games. Apparently there is no excitement at church that compares with that of the NBA, especially when the Chicago Bulls are in the playoffs!

Why this monotony, this lack of excitement?

It is not easy being faithful to rituals, even if we do understand their meaning. Nor is there much excitement in trying to live up to a moral standard we know we can't meet. One person told me, "I find myself expending my energy for church, but I just don't get anything in return."

This is not a new problem. By nature, we humans define our religion by what we expect ourselves and others to do. And "doing" becomes wearisome. Boring—at times, boring indeed.

In New Testament times, there was a group of religious leaders who weighed out their religious commitments to the last gram. They had more red tape than you could measure; some regulations defined other regulations. Their religious system seemed designed for failure. No matter how much you did, there was something you either forgot to do or more you should have done. Not only was the excitement gone, so also was the hope of the common man, who couldn't even remember the regulations, much less keep them.

These religious leaders were the Pharisees, good folks in many ways but specialists in misusing the Old Testament law, interpreting it as a set of complicated rules rather than as a means to experience God's grace. No wonder Jesus said of them, "They tie up heavy loads, and lay them on men's shoulders; but they themselves are unwilling to move them with so much as a finger" (Matthew 23:4). They loved to strap religion on people's backs and see them squirm.

But one of these men, bless him, was so desperate to find reality in his religion that he came to Christ to ask some important questions that just might help him get the load of religion off his back. We have to commend him, because he knew how critical Christ was of his self-righteous crowd. But then, finding the narrow way that leads to life is not always easy.

This man was Nicodemus, a Pharisee who sat on the highest legislative body in Judaism. He shared a seat on the bench, representing the final court of appeal for the enforcement of Jewish law. He was a part of that brotherhood, one of those who thought themselves a cut above everyone else. He was a religious man among religious men.

Interestingly, though he had *rules,* he did not have *reality;* though admired as *good,* he did not have *God.* No matter how pious he was on the outside, he was rotting within. In fact, though he didn't know it yet, his religion was more of a hindrance than a help.

He came to Christ by night, possibly because he did not want to be seen conversing with the Man he was supposed to hate. Christ, you remember, embarrassed the pious Pharisees by bypassing their hocus-pocus and getting down to the issues of the heart.

The Judean night was no darker than Nicodemus's soul, spiritually speaking. Later, he would leave the darkness and come into the clear light of day—but that's getting ahead of the story.

Let us summarize the conversation as recorded in John 3:1–7, beginning with a question from Nicodemus.

"Rabbi, we know that You have come from God as a teacher; for no one can do these signs that You do unless God is with him."

Jesus answered, "Truly, truly, I say to you, unless one is born again, he cannot see the kingdom of God."

Nicodemus replied, "How can a man be born when he is old? He cannot enter a second time into his mother's womb and be born, can he?"

Jesus answered, "Truly, truly, I say to you, unless one is born of water and the Spirit, he cannot enter into the kingdom of God. That which is born of the flesh is flesh; and that which is born of the Spirit is spirit. Do not marvel that I said to you, 'You must be born again.'"

WE MUST BE BORN AGAIN?

What did Christ mean by the expression *born again?* We use it today to mean "remade." In today's newspaper there is an article about a dilapidated tombstone that was restored, and the headline says it is "Born Again." A politician who switches from the Republicans to the Democrats is said to be "born again" (or is it the other way around?). Or perhaps an actor has reinvented himself, and the press now says he is "born again."

We had better find out what Christ meant by the term, because He said no one can see heaven without it. It really means "to be born from above." Christ was speaking of the work of the Holy Spirit within us; he was helping us grasp a miracle that only God can do.

Another word for the new birth is the fifty-dollar term *regeneration*. But even that word is not as difficult as it sounds. It just means "the act or process of being generated again." The Bible uses both words to refer to the same work of God by which He implants spiritual life within our souls. It is the creation within us of a God-like nature. This act changes us fundamentally. We are "new creations" in Christ.

Why do we have to be born again? God had warned Adam and Eve, "In the day that you eat from [the tree of the knowledge of good and evil] you shall surely die" (Genesis 2:17). And die they did. Awash with shame and regret, they tried to run away from God. They were banished from the Garden, their intellects became darkened, and the communication lines between them and God were jammed. We inherited their sin, and though we did not lose the ability to reason, we did lose the ability to reason our way to God. Worse yet, we were left with no way to repair the damage.

Adam and Eve began to die physically on the day they sinned, and they would have died eternally—that is, forever separated from God—if God had not intervened. Just as a short circuit causes a light bulb to go out, so sin tripped the switch. Morally and spiritually, the human race (that's us, folks) was plunged into darkness.

To be "born again," or "regenerated," means that the circuit breakers are repaired and we are put back into contact with God. God renews our spirit and gives us a new nature; eventually, in the resurrection, we will receive a new body. We're talking about a serious transformation!

To put it differently, just as our physical birth made us members of our earthly family, so being born spiritually is necessary to make us members of our heavenly family. And just as a newborn baby has only a future and no past, so God comes to forgive our past and give us a new future. No wonder Christ said, "Unless one is born again, . . . he cannot enter into the kingdom of God" (John 3:3, 5)!

Nicodemus didn't get it. He heard the words *being born,* and his mind honed in on obstetrics. That's why he asked, "How can a man be born when he is old? He cannot enter a second time into his mother's womb and be born, can he?"

Christ replied, "Truly, truly, I say to you, unless one is born of water and the Spirit, he cannot enter into the kingdom of God." This birth has nothing to do with your mother, but it has everything to do with your Father— your Father in heaven, that is.

We must be "born of water and the Spirit." You probably know that many people see the word *water* and think that Christ is referring to baptism. But the word *baptism* is nowhere in this passage. I would like to suggest respectfully that baptism would not have crossed Nicodemus's mind—and remember, Christ expected Nicodemus to already know the things they were speaking about that evening (see verse 10).

If baptism were really necessary to enter the kingdom of heaven, then virtually no one in Old Testament times would have qualified. Baptism began with John the Baptist during Christ's ministry, but it was not practiced by the Jews. Yes, the priests were to wash themselves with water, but that was not their entrance into the kingdom of heaven. God never makes His salvation dependent on a ritual.

Nicodemus would have known that in the Old Testament *water* and *Spirit* are often joined to refer to spiritual refreshment that comes from God. A passage from Ezekiel would probably have come to mind: "Then I will sprinkle clean water on you, and you will be clean; I will cleanse you from all your filthiness and from all your idols. Moreover, I will give you a new heart and put a new spirit within you; and I will remove the heart of stone from your flesh and give you a heart of flesh" (Ezekiel 36:25–26).

Whenever *water* is used symbolically in the Old Testament, it always refers to renewal or cleansing, especially when it is joined with the word *Spirit.* There is a "pouring out" of the Spirit referred to in many passages (see, for example, Isaiah 32:15; 44:3–5). When the Holy Spirit does His work, there is the miracle of transformation but also the miracle of cleansing. The cleansing of the Holy Spirit does what water can never do.

There is a second reason to think Christ was using water as a symbol of the Holy Spirit's work. He did not say that we must be "born of water and born of Spirit," as if there were two separate births. He said, rather, that we must be born "of water and the Spirit." Water and Spirit are joined together, but there is only *one* birth, the one that is "from above." That is why the phrase is sometimes translated "born of water *even* the Spirit." This new birth is done by God without human assistance.

Keep this in mind: Justification and the new birth happen at the same time. They are two different blessings that come to us when we experience saving faith. Although they cannot be separated, they must be distinguished. Justification happens *outside* of us; it is God's declaration in heaven that we are as righteous as Christ.

The new birth happens *inside* of us. We are given spiritual life and are connected to God.

CHARACTERISTICS OF THE NEW BIRTH

Christ contrasted our physical birth with our spiritual birth, as He explained to Nicodemus: "That which is born of the flesh is flesh, and that which is born of the Spirit is spirit" (John 3:6). Flesh begets flesh, and Spirit begets Spirit.

You'll be surprised, I think, at what a great miracle the new birth really is. Clearly, this is something we cannot do, but, thanks be, God can.

The Work of Our Heavenly Father

We were born the first time as a result of the sperm of our father uniting with the ovum of our mother to produce a zygote. I inherited the characteristics of my parents but also their nature (a sinful nature, I might add).

Just so, two elements come together to cause us to be born into God's family. The Word of God (the gospel) unites with the Spirit of God to perform the miracle of God, the new birth. Listen to the words of Peter: "For you have been born again not of seed which is perishable but imperishable, that is, through the living and abiding word of God" (1 Peter 1:23).

Our physical birth was of corruptible seed; our spiritual birth is of incorruptible seed. Our parents were incapable of cleansing the line of corruption we inherited. But the second birth, since it is of *in*corruptible seed, did what the first birth couldn't do.

On October 3, 1941, I was born into my family, thanks to my father and mother. Fourteen years later, after I had become so aware of my sinfulness that I could scarcely sleep, God graciously gave me the gift of faith, and I was reborn into my spiritual family. The Word of God combined with the Spirit of God to beget new life in me.

Two humans can beget a child in their own likeness, morally and physically (we've all marveled at how strikingly similar to his father or mother a child can look). Just so, God begets us in His own likeness. Don't get me wrong. God always remains God, and we always remain human. But when we are born again, we do receive His nature. *We don't become perfect in our everyday living, but we are made different.*

Neither you nor I can give the new birth to anyone. We are begotten by God alone, without human assistance. There are many things we can do, but bringing about the new birth is not one of them. When God regenerates, He is acting through the Word and the Spirit. The new birth is a direct act of omnipotence.

That should clinch it for us. Paul wrote, "Therefore if any man is in Christ, he is a new creature; the old things passed away; behold, new things have come" (2 Corinthians 5:17). Scientists have done many wonderful things, but one thing they have never done is to create so much as a single molecule. Creation is God's work, and we can only stand in awe of His power. He created the universe ex nihilo, that is, out of nothing. Even if we had been living on the day when the heavens and the earth were created, He would not have needed us to make His job easier. There was no need for our help because it was just "a bit much" for the Almighty. No, He acted alone— and with good reason.

When we are "born again," God creates within us a new nature that was not there before His intervention. Light was also created by divine fiat. Just so, the spiritual light that produces the new birth is the sovereign work of God. "For God, who said, 'Light shall shine out of darkness,' is the One who has shone in our hearts to give the light of the knowledge of the glory of God in the face of Christ" (2 Corinthians 4:6–7). The shaft of light that causes us to be reborn has to come from God alone. He acted alone, creating it ex nihilo.

In the second chapter, I used the apostle Paul's analogy of resurrection to illustrate salvation. When Christ came to the tomb of Lazarus, He didn't expect help from the disciples, nor from Lazarus. He didn't say, "Now Lazarus, you should at least lift your elbow if you want Me to raise you from the dead!"

Once the miracle happened and Lazarus staggered out of the cave in which he had been buried, the disciples were able to remove the grave clothes. They were able to get something for Lazarus to eat. They could help him get reoriented into earthly existence. But when Lazarus lay in the grave, they could but watch as Christ did what only God can do.

Of course, when God saves us, there is one difference. We do agree to let Him do His work; we do exercise trust in what Christ has done. Whereas inanimate nature has neither mind, emotion, nor will, we have all three. And yet, our response is really the result of God's working in our hearts. God makes us conscious of our need for Christ; God gives us the ability to believe. Salvation is His work from start to finish.

The creation of the world and the creation of light are, of course, great miracles. The new birth is different in that it doesn't affect the whole universe; the new nature within is not as great as the starry heavens; the light of the mind is not as blinding as the light of the sun. And our resurrection unto life is not as spectacular as Lazarus staggering out of the tomb.

And yet the new birth may be an even greater miracle! In the creation of the universe we see only the awesome *power* of God; in the miracle of regeneration we see the *mercy* and *grace* of God. The stars are the work of His fingers, symbolically speaking, but salvation is the work of His arm. God created matter and then put it in its place; but when He saved us, He had to overcome our blindness and the stubbornness of our wills. He brought us into agreement with what He was doing.

Back in 1954, soloist George Beverly Shea of the Billy Graham team sang this song to a packed crowd in London's Harringay Arena:

> *It took a miracle to put the stars in place,*
> *It took a miracle to hang the world in space;*
> *But when He saved my soul,*
> *Cleansed and made me whole,*
> *It took a miracle of love and grace!*[1]

An English lady, who had obviously misunderstood the words, came to Shea later and indignantly remarked, "What do you mean by saying 'it took *America* to put the stars in place'?!"

America has done some wonderful things, has even trained astronomers who have diligently studied the stars, but, as yet, none of them has been able to create even one new star. We have put men on the moon, but only God could have created the moon. We must sharply distinguish between what we can do and what God can do. Only God can cause us to be reborn from above.

Other religions try to make men better, but only Christianity makes men alive. The new birth reconnects the switch that was turned off when Adam and Eve sinned in the Garden of Eden. The miracle is all one-sided. Charles Wesley understood God's sovereign work in salvation when he wrote this hymn we love to sing:

Long my imprisoned spirit lay
Fast bound in sin and nature's night;
Thine eye diffused a quickening ray,
I woke, the dungeon flamed with light;
My chains fell off, my heart was free;
I rose, went forth, and followed thee.

We are the prisoners; God is the liberator. He shines light into the dungeon, cuts the chains, and tells us we are free. If He did not act, we would be lost forever.

The Will of Our Heavenly Father

Now I'm going to say something that might make you feel uncomfortable, but stay with me. Did you choose to be born physically? No, that was a choice made by your parents. (I've met some people who have complained about the fact that they arrived on earth without having a say in the matter!)

Who made the choice that you should be reborn spiritually? If I told you that our Father in heaven made the choice, you might complain that that isn't fair. And what is more, it seems "obvious" that you made the decision. And, I must agree, it was your decision, for no one was ever born again against his will. Anyone who desires to be born again can be.

Yet listen to the words of Christ to Nicodemus: "The wind blows where it wishes and you hear the sound of it, but do not know where it comes from and where it is going; so is everyone who is born of the Spirit" (John 3:8). Christ makes a connection between the breeze that He and Nicodemus heard above the roof of the house and the work of the Holy Spirit.

Catch this: In Greek, the word for *wind* is the same as the word that is translated *Spirit* in this passage (only the context tells us how it should be translated). Wind is beyond the control of men and is often unpredictable, blowing in one part of the country but not in another. It is also mysterious. Weathermen can now make rather accurate predictions short-term, but they cannot predict the speed of the wind a year from today, nor can they tell how many tornadoes will develop next spring. Similarly, the work of the Spirit is beyond human explanation, and the Spirit does as He wills.

Although I memorized John 1:12–13 many years ago, I did not take the time until quite recently to think through the meaning of the verses. The text reads, "But as many as received Him, to them He gave the right to become children of God, even to those who believe in His name, who were born not of blood, nor of the will of the flesh, nor of the will of man, but of God" (John 1:12–13). Did you notice how John credits the work of this new birth wholly to God? He says that we were "not [born] of blood"; that is, we are not born again by human lineage. No one is ever born again simply because his parents were Christians. God has many children, but no grandchildren.

Being born again is not a decision our parents can make for us, nor are we born again by being reared in a fine church or a pious family. We don't "catch" the new birth from someone else in the same way we might "catch" a virus. God must act or we are lost.

John continues: Nor are we born again by "the will of the flesh," which means that we were not the ones who came seeking for God. Finally, the new birth was not by "the will of man, but of God." John here has eliminated any possibility of tracing our new birth to ourselves, our family background, or even our own decisions.

James confirms this. "In the exercise of His will He brought us forth by the word of truth, so that we might be, as it were, the first fruits among His creatures" (James

1:18). We are born again because God exercised His will and chose to show mercy to us. What I once thought was the result of my will turns out to be the result of God's will!

I can hear a chorus of objections. "What do you mean, 'God made the decision'? I am born again because I chose to be! And what about those who were not chosen!"

This is not the place to answer all those questions, except to say that here's what happens: God brings many circumstances into our lives, perhaps a Christian family or Christian friends, and we become aware of the good news about Christ's coming to die for sinners. As our curiosity grows, so does the recognition that we are sinners who need to be saved. We are given the conviction that if there is any hope at all for us, it must be found in Christ. We finally see that we must choose to put our faith in Christ as our sin-bearer. At that moment, God completes the new birth within us.

But don't miss the point. The reason we choose Christ is that God worked in our hearts to bring us to that point of trust. The decision that I would be born physically was made entirely without me; the decision that I would be reborn into God's kingdom was made with my consent to be sure, although my exercise of faith was God-given. Salvation is entirely God's work.

In New Testament times, there lived a woman named Lydia. When she heard Paul preach, "the Lord opened her heart" (Acts 16:14). She didn't open her own heart. Paul didn't open her heart. God did what only He can do. He showed her the truth and gave her the ability to believe on Christ.

Have no fear. The invitation to believe on Christ is extended to everyone. No one who wishes to be born again is ever denied the privilege. Some respond; some do not.

Those who have the desire to receive the gift of God's grace do so because that desire has been implanted there by God. But by nature, we do not seek God. God seeks us.

The Way of Our Heavenly Father

Obviously, we cannot cause someone to be born again. And yet, in the history of the church, people have often thought they could. That is one reason there are so many people who claim to be Christians but cannot give evidence that God has done a miracle in their hearts. They assume they are saved because they have a certificate to prove it.

Let's take infant baptism. Many people regard it simply as a form of dedication, a sign of God's covenant within the church and their own family. But others believe that baptism washes away sin and makes the infant "a child of God." In fact, I remember reading one liturgy that says, "It is through the waters of baptism that we are reborn."

This teaching assumes that the new birth is under our control, that the decision to be born again can be made for us by our parents or even by the ministers of God. We can thus be born again without any knowledge of our sins and our need to trust Christ as our substitute.

Others believe they are born again through adult baptism or by belonging to the right church. They are taught that faith in Christ plus some other man-made ritual will bring about the miracle they need. Not until man acts, they say, does God act.

Is it any wonder that there are so many people who have been baptized but have no desire to walk in obedience to God's Word? They might be told that they are Christians but wonder why life is so boring, so powerless. Or they might continue to work hard to be saved, believing that if baptism is necessary, other rituals might be necessary too. Like Nicodemus, they might be very religious, but also very lost.

And what shall we say of "decisional regeneration" practiced so widely in evangelical churches today? A potential convert is told he must know that he is a sinner, pray a prescribed prayer to "accept Christ into his heart," and answer a few questions. Then he is told that he is now a Christian. No wonder there are many people who say they are trusting Christ as their Savior but only *think* they are.

This kind of teaching is often accompanied by invitations to come forward at evangelistic meetings. The impression is given, even if not stated, that coming to Christ means walking down an aisle or signing a card. Although most who use this kind of appeal know that coming to Christ and coming forward in a meeting are not the same thing, they do give the impression that the first step for sinners is to walk to the front, perhaps to the platform or the altar.

An invitation might be properly used if those who come forward do so to have their questions answered, receive prayer, or be given counsel. But by confusing coming to Christ with coming to an altar, many people have been misguided. Some think they are saved because they came forward and did all that they were told. Others think they cannot be saved because they are too shy to walk in front of a crowd.

Getting the chicken out of the egg can be dangerous. Although the need to believe is urgent, we cannot put pressure on people to be converted until they are ready. We must present the gospel and let God do what we cannot. Luther, with perhaps a bit of exaggeration, said that we must descend into hell before we can ascend into heaven. That was his way of saying that we should not get people saved until we get them lost.

Let us never forget that sinners cannot regenerate themselves. Let us also remember that a sinner can pray the right prayer, sign the right card, answer the right questions, and go to the right altar without having believed. To be saved, a person must transfer his trust to Christ alone and accept Him as his sin-bearer. Only such faith is evidence that God has regenerated him.

The great preacher Charles Haddon Spurgeon not only refused to give altar calls but even discouraged people from coming to be counseled in an inquiry room. He feared that they might be lured into a fictitious confidence that their conversion actually took place. He urged them, "Go to your God at once, even where you now are. Cast yourself on Christ, ere you stir an inch!"

Better that people be urged to seek God on their own, believe the promises, and ask God to confirm that they have transferred their trust to Christ. Better to let doubt (which is the subject of a future chapter) do its work.

By now you might be wondering what good it is to witness to the gospel of Christ if salvation is in God's hands and not ours. What part, if any, do we play in helping men and women believe?

The prophet Ezekiel was standing in a valley of dry bones, which symbolized the spiritual deadness of the nation Israel. The physicians of Israel would have been able to classify the bones, but they couldn't give them life. The mighty men of Israel would have been able to move the bones, but in doing so they would only succeed in transferring deadness from one part of the valley to another.

There *was*, however, something the prophet could do. He could preach to the bones and trust God to do what only God could do, namely, give them the miracle of life. So he preached, "O dry bones, hear the word of the Lord" (Ezekiel 37:4). Within a short time, he heard a rattling, and the bones came together, bone joined to bone. Then flesh grew around the bones. When the bodies were fully formed, he prayed, and breath came to the corpses and they stood on their feet as a great army.

Just so, we have the responsibility of sharing the good news of the gospel. We are to pray, discuss, and communicate. But we know better than to think that we ourselves can give life. We trust God to do what only He can do. And we also know that if He doesn't do it, it won't get done.

The new birth is instantaneous. It happens at a specific moment of time. Though there are many events that lead up to it, once it happens it is sudden and complete. We have passed "out of death into life" (John 5:24). It is supernatural, instantaneous, invisible, and eternal. We are "delivered . . . from the domain of darkness, and transferred . . . to the kingdom of His beloved Son" (Colossians 1:13).

The new birth is never repeated. Medieval theology taught that conversion was a process, a never-ending, often tortuous experience. The route to perfection was long and fraught with many possibilities for failure.

Not so. A healthy child is born complete, everything in place. The baby will have ten toes, ten fingers, and even little fingernails. Its ears will be perfect, a tribute to God's creative ability. In the same way, when we are born spiritually, everything is in place: we are God's children, partakers of the divine nature. "And in Him," says Paul, "you have been made complete" (Colossians 2:10). Now our responsibility is to grow. That's what newborn babies do.

The dry bones are resurrected in a moment of time, but their service to God continues after that. An old but true saying goes like this: "I have been saved, I am being saved, and some day I shall be fully saved." Though we are raised from death to life in a moment of time and are therefore "saved" when we believe on Christ, we are also "being saved" in the sense that God continues the work He has begun in our hearts. And, of course, in the future, when we arrive in heaven, we "will be saved" completely from even the presence of sin.

Only Christ could raise Lazarus, but once he was out of the grave, he was able to serve God. Just so, once we have been born again we must grow in our faith, not in order to be fit for heaven but because we want to serve Christ acceptably on earth.

We cannot take our blind eyes and make them see; we cannot give life to our spiritually dead natures; and we cannot cause our deaf ears to hear. Even so, we are commanded to believe, to repent that we might be saved. When we do, we know it is a miracle of God. And, as Ezekiel learned, if we share the message of life with others, the rest is in God's hands.

THE LOOK THAT SAVES

If you are somewhat rattled at God's sovereignty in the miracle of the new birth, you can take comfort in this: you can discover whether or not you are among those who will receive the benefits of His gracious work. What you must do is trust Christ alone, which confirms God's work in your heart.

Christ reminded Nicodemus of the Old Testament story of how Moses put a bronze serpent on a pole and invited those who had contracted a deadly disease to look at it. If they did so, this act of faith would bring about healing. These are Christ's words:

> And as Moses lifted up the serpent in the wilderness, even so must the Son of Man be lifted up; that whoever believes may in Him have eternal life. For God so loved the world, that He gave His only begotten Son, that whoever believes in Him should not perish, but have eternal life. (John 3:14–16)

Just imagine what happened that day in the wilderness. Many people complained, saying that this invitation didn't make sense. How could looking at a serpent (or any object) that wasn't even touching the sick folks be a remedy for the disease within them?

A good question, but the fact is that God chose to do a miracle; He chose to act on behalf of those who had the faith to obey the command of Moses. Just so, we look to Christ for the remedy of the disease called sin. We do not understand how Someone who died and was raised two thousand years ago can do a permanent miracle in our hearts, but God says that if we look, we will live.

This look is a humble recognition of our sinfulness, a decision to receive Christ's work for ourselves. It is a look that embraces the wonder of God's love for us and invites Him to declare us righteous and make us one of His children forever. This faith is a ticket to the narrow way that leads to life.

For some, this act results in an immediate experience of peace and freedom from guilt. For others, it is a quiet moment with little emotion or deep feeling. For all, it is the beginning of a whole new relationship with God. The broken communication lines have been restored. At last we know God.

This was not the last contact Nicodemus had with Christ. After Jesus died on the cross, His body needed burial, so Joseph of Arimathea came to take His body away: "And Nicodemus came also, who had first come to Him by night; bringing a mixture of myrrh and aloes, about a hundred pounds weight. And so they took the body of Jesus, and bound it in linen wrappings with the spices, as is the burial custom of the Jews" (John 19:39–40). This was a bold step for a man who was a Jewish leader. Christ was supposed to be his enemy, but Nicodemus cared for Him as a friend.

We can be quite sure that only someone who had experienced the new birth would have had the courage to be counted along with Christ's disciples, risking ostracism and even death. Nicodemus had moved from opinions to convictions, from death to life. He came to Jesus by night, but later he identified with Christ in broad daylight.

Can religion be boring? Yes, as long as God appears distant and removed from our experience. As long as Nicodemus lived at the level of ritual, he found his religion empty; when he came to faith in Christ, his life became full. Of course, we can still fall into boring routines even after we have been born again. But now we do have a reason to be excited. Life has new meaning. Even religious people must be born again.

And now I ask you: Are you, my friend, born again? Even while you have been reading this chapter, God just might have "opened your heart." If so, let Him finish what He has begun. Go to God right now. Accept Christ as the one who died for you. Believe and be saved.

Nicodemus needed this miracle. So do we.

NOTE

1. Words and music by John W. Peterson. Copyright 1948, renewed by John W. Peterson Music Co. All rights reserved. Used by permission.

CHAPTER FIVE

ℋELD IN GOD'S HANDS

S o *that's* what you believe!"

The man spit out his words like a chess player who was about to move his queen and declare, "Checkmate!"

"If *that's* what you believe," he continued, "then I can receive God's grace once for all and then live like the Devil and still go to heaven!" It was a deal that sounded too good to be true. The idea of having a reservation in heaven that could not be canceled no matter how he lived was appealing indeed.

So is it true that salvation once received cannot be lost?

Let's ask Ted Turner.

"I was saved seven or eight times, but when I lost my faith I felt better about it," Turner said when speaking to a group of humanists. He was raised, he said, in an extremely religious environment, including six years in a Christian prep school with Bible training and daily chapel services and regular meetings with evangelists.

He continued, "With no other influences in my life at the time and the way it was pounded into us so much, I think I was saved many times." He said he even considered missionary work, but when his younger sister got sick, "I prayed and nothing happened, of course." When she died, Turner said, he couldn't understand why this loving God he had heard about would allow someone who was innocent to suffer.

Turner still was not finished:

> I thought about it and said to myself, I'm not sure I want any part of this; if God is love and all powerful, why does He allow all these things to happen? This interpretation that it's just God's will . . . well, I can't get enthusiastic about that. I began to lose my faith and the more I lost it the better I felt![1]

So there you have it. Here is a man who was saved "seven or eight times," but no one can accuse him of being a believer today. He represents many others who apparently were at one time "born again" but lost their faith along the way.

The question of whether a born-again believer can lose his faith and be lost in hell forever has been controversial in the history of the church. I cannot pretend to settle hundreds of years of disagreement in a single chapter, but I can give you a few of the reasons why some of us think the Bible makes the matter very clear. And I might also have an explanation for the Ted Turners of this world.

Of course I know that some people think we are saved only as long as we keep ourselves "in the faith." Often this is based on the depressing idea that if we die with sins that have not been confessed, God undoes all the work that He did for us. Our justification is canceled; the new birth is undone.

I sat next to a man on the plane who was taught this as a child. He was afraid he had committed some sin that he had not confessed. If he died during the night, he would be damned. When he reached his teens, he realized that he could never "stay saved," so he decided to leave the faith until some future date, possibly just before he died. "I'm on furlough from living the Christian life," he told me.

Harry Ironside, for many years the pastor of Moody Church in Chicago, said he met a man who claimed he had been saved ninety-nine times. (Actually, if he believed he lost his salvation every time he sinned, I think the total would be much higher!)

A woman who was brought up with this kind of confusing theology said that in her church the town drunk got saved every Sunday morning and was drunk every Sunday evening. One day the pastor said to him, "Next Sunday we ought to shoot you right after you get saved!"

He was joking, of course, but you get the point. If you believe a person gets "unsaved" every time he falls into sin, you would be doing the man a favor to shoot him the moment he's saved. Better that than to die tomorrow unsaved.

Others say that we lose our salvation only when we commit a willful sin and are no longer in a "state of grace." This might happen through moral failure or turning away from the Bible into serious doctrinal error. If you are convinced of this, then all those who commit suicide are lost in hell. At any rate, the argument goes, we can't be sure today that we will be saved tomorrow.

I've even known some people to say that we should never comfort others with the thought that we can be sure of heaven because they will become complacent and "live like the Devil." They fear that people will get a ticket to heaven and then be careless, doing just as they please. And we have all met individuals who appear to be doing just that.

But is that a good reason to abandon a doctrine that is taught in the Scriptures? And what is more, I want to show that our security can be motivation for living a committed Christian life.

SAVED TODAY, SAVED FOREVER

You have already guessed that I'm going to insist that God not only takes the initiative in saving us but is committed to those whom He saves, committed to the very end. He will bring all of His children home to heaven.

The Bible is a consistent book and cannot contradict itself. I believe that it overwhelmingly confirms that a true believer will never be lost. The work of God in the human heart is both miraculous and irreversible. Salvation, as we have learned, is God's mighty work. Our decision to accept Christ is rooted in His sovereign plans and intentions.

When the Holy Spirit comes to take up residence in our hearts we are "sealed until the day of redemption" (Ephesians 4:32). We are like a letter mailed on earth that is guaranteed to arrive in heaven. God is both the sender and the recipient. We can say that He seals us here; and despite the turbulence en route, no one can open the seal until we have arrived safely. And God will be there to do it.

Let's plunge in and take a careful look at a passage of Scripture that paints a rather complete picture of the panorama of God's purposes. You might be surprised at the detailed attention God gives to those who become members of His family.

Just stay with me, and we'll take a fast ride over some interesting theological ideas to show that God will never disown His children. They will never be lost in a child custody battle; they were purchased by His Son, and He is committed to keeping them even when they misbehave.

FIVE UNBREAKABLE LINKS

You've seen a building under construction: boards, bricks and steel girders are stacked close to the freshly dug excavation site. Day after day the work crew pieces the material together. Gradually, a new building emerges from the unconnected haphazard materials.

How does such a transformation take place? By following a blueprint. Before construction ever began, an architect, or perhaps several of them, spent countless hours drawing plans that included everything from the apex of the roof to the electrical outlets.

If humans are smart enough to know that a building cannot be constructed without a master plan—if we have to choose every brick and window to fit the blueprint —we can just as easily see that God would not have created us without a specific plan in mind. We were chosen and designed for a purpose.

God was already preparing for our arrival on planet Earth long before we arrived on the scene. In the Scriptures, the curtain is pushed back, and we are allowed to peek into the plans and aspirations of Almighty God. There we discover we are not an afterthought.

In Romans 8:29–30, the apostle Paul uses five verbs to describe God's great works on our behalf. Read the passage. If some of the terms are unfamiliar to you, don't be discouraged. We'll define them in a moment.

> For whom He foreknew, He also predestined to become conformed to the image of His Son, that He might be the first-born among many brethren; and whom He predestined, these He also called; and whom He called, these He

also justified; and whom He justified, these He also glorified. (Romans 8:29–30)

You have just read a passage containing five verbs that form links in an unbreakable chain. God begins, says Paul, with those "whom He foreknew" and ends with those whom He has "glorified." There are no loopholes; there is no possibility that one of God's children can fall through the cracks. All of them belong to Him in the beginning, and they are still His in eternity.

"Whom He Foreknew"

This means much more than the fact that God knew about us ahead of time. It means that He "foreloved us." Long before we arrived on planet Earth He had already chosen us to be His; we were already cherished.

The Old Testament uses the phrase *to know* with the same meaning. The King James Version of Amos 3:2 says, "You only have I known of all the families of the earth." Interestingly, the *New American Standard Bible* translates the phrase as "You only have I chosen among all the families of the earth." And that, of course, is the idea. Perhaps the best way to translate it is to say that those who are foreknown are those upon whom God has "set His affection."

If you are a born-again Christian, you can stop right here and thank God that you mean so much to Him!

"He Also Predestined"

The word *predestined* means "to mark out ahead of time." Sometimes it was used by town surveyors, who arrived long before the people to mark out where the streets and buildings would be. In the same way, God mapped out ahead of time that we would be "conformed to the image of His Son." His plan will be accomplished, for God delights to honor His Son by giving Him "brothers." Of course, we will never be like Christ in His essence, but we "shall be like Him, because we shall see Him just as He is" (1 John 3:2).

"He Also Called"

Third is the verb *called*. When we are "called," we experience the conviction of the Holy Spirit and respond to the gospel of Christ. This particular call is effectual; that is, it accomplishes its intended result. The Holy Spirit enlightens our minds, opens our hearts, makes us aware of our need, and gives us the ability to put our faith in Christ.

When we transfer our trust to Christ, we think that the decision is entirely ours and that our destiny is in our own hands. But, as we've been learning, we must trace our decision back to the inscrutable and certain plan of our heavenly Father.

"He Also Justified"

Since we discussed justification in a previous chapter, I need only point out here that this means more than the fact that our sins are forgiven. Justification means that I have been declared as righteous as Christ Himself and will be considered as such for all of eternity.

"He Also Glorified"

Finally, we come to the word *glorified*. Look into the mirror, and we will all agree that not a one of us looks very glorified in the here and now. Glorification, that is, receiving our new bodies and sinless natures, seems so far off that we wonder what it all will mean. Today we are not glorified, and everyone around us knows it. And yet this is the goal toward which we are moving.

The first two links in this chain begin in eternity past, the third is on earth, and the last two end in heaven. Notice that God is the subject of each of these verbs; that means He does all the acting. We are the objects; we do all the receiving. We are "acted upon" by the providential hand of God. And what He begins He finishes.

What is more, every one of these verbs is in the past tense! Even the word *glorified* is considered as something that God has already done. God writes the future as if it were history. Looked at from His point of view, we are already in heaven. Someone has said that this is a "daring anticipation." What a stupendous guarantee!

Those who were "foreknown" in eternity past are the same ones who end up glorified. Neither Satan nor they themselves can cause God to withdraw His love and faithfulness. He will bring them to where He says they already are!

CHRIST OUR ATTORNEY

If you are out of breath trying to grasp how much attention God is pleased to give us, there is more. Paul himself seems to be at a loss as to how to continue. Immediately after listing the five "links," he writes, "What then shall we say to these things? If God is for us, who is against us?" (Romans 8:31). Though he wonders what to say, he does not stop there. Under the guidance of the Holy Spirit, He continues to assure us of God's faithfulness toward His people.

He visualizes a courtroom scene. "Who will bring a charge against God's elect? God is the one who justifies; who is the one who condemns? Christ Jesus is He who died, yes, rather who was raised, who is at the right hand of God, who also intercedes for us" (verses 33–34).

This is not a municipal court; nor is this the Supreme Court of the United States. It is the Supreme Court of the

Universe. God is hearing cases, and if we use our imaginations, we can listen to the proceedings.

Picture yourself as the defendant. You are at one end of a long table. The Devil, who is in cahoots with your conscience, is at the other end. Seated between the two of you is your attorney, Christ, who has chosen to take up your cause. On an elevated throne across from the table is the Judge of all the earth, God Almighty.

The Devil gives his opening arguments. He gives reasons (plenty of them) you should be barred from heaven. What makes it embarrassing is that he does not just mention some rather common sins you have committed but exposes nasty secrets that you thought were safely hidden. Like it or not, your dirty laundry is strung out across the courtroom. Added to your shame is the fact that what is being said is true. You cannot put your own spin on the details because you are in the presence of God, who has knowledge of all things both actual and possible. You are already embarrassed, but there is more to come.

Satan shouts the damning conclusion, "This person cannot be a member of God's family. He must be cast away from the presence of God forever." In his closing arguments he says that if the Judge does not agree with his conclusion, more accusations are in the offing. There is a briefcase with lists of sins that have not yet been mentioned. Indeed, a U-Haul® trailer full of sins is parked outside the door.

What are your options? You cannot deny the accusations. God knows better, and so do you. It does no good to compare yourself to others, arguing that you are not as great a sinner as those who lived next door. You are being tried—you alone—a solitary human being in the Courtroom of the Universe.

What you once considered a speck of sin that was easily

rationalized now looks like a mountain. The excuses you were planning to use evaporate like dew in hot sun.

Your best option, or more accurately, your *only* option, is to turn to your attorney. You let Christ handle the accusations for you. You tell Him, "This is all Yours."

Christ agrees with the accusations but points out that His death settled your account. He announces, loud enough for the cringing Devil to hear, that this particular sinner has been declared just as righteous as God. And the Judge has already agreed to accept the terms of the acquittal.

Who would dare impeach the Judge? Who would dare call you a sinner if God has chosen to call you a saint? That is why Paul says, "Who will bring a charge against God's elect? God is the one who justifies; who is the one who condemns? Christ Jesus is He who died, yes, rather who was raised, who is at the right hand of God, who also intercedes for us" (Romans 8:33–34).

Christ's presence in heaven guarantees that those who are His will not fall under the judgment of God. There is no legal loophole by which God is able to get out of His pledge to save those who have believed on His beloved Son. He can't, and He won't.

Even as you read this book, if you are a believer in Christ, you already have taken up residency in heaven. We are "in Christ," and Christ is at the right hand of God the Father. We cannot be thrown out of heaven unless Christ Himself were to be thrown out. If we have really believed (what this means will be discussed in the next chapter), we can be sure that we will spend eternity with God.

But couldn't something happen that would cut us off from Christ? For us skeptics, Paul now lists all those things that will attempt to drive a wedge between us and God. Just when we seem to be free of guilt, Satan will want to make us doubt God's love. Or we may have a tragedy in our family, and the first thing that crosses our mind is *If God loves us, why this?* There are times when we are deprived and times when we might be persecuted for our faith in Christ. And when the economy goes belly-up and we lose everything we have worked for, it is easy to conclude that God really doesn't care for us after all.

Listen to how Paul raises these issues and then answers them:

> Who shall separate us from the love of Christ? Shall tribulation, or distress, or persecution, or famine, or nakedness, or peril, or sword? Just as it is written, "For Thy sake we are being put to death all day long; we were considered as sheep to be slaughtered." But in all these things we overwhelmingly conquer through Him who loved us. For I am convinced that neither death, nor life, nor angels, nor principalities, nor things present, nor things to come, nor powers, nor height, nor depth, nor any other created thing, shall be able to separate us from the love of God, which is in Christ Jesus our Lord. (Romans 8:35–39)

What can separate us from the love of Christ? Death can't do it; life with all of its hassles can't do it; angels can't; Satan can't; present calamities can't; future catastrophes can't; political authorities can't; nor can anything that has been overlooked in this list!

CHRIST OUR SHEPHERD

When Paul wrote, "Just as it is written, 'For Thy sake we are being put to death all day long; we were considered as sheep to be slaughtered'" (verse 36), he was quoting Psalm 44:22. Although God's people are often mistreated, maligned, and misunderstood, the Shepherd does not abandon them. Even if they should be slaughtered, this Shepherd preserves them throughout eternity.

Paul's point, of course, is that despite the harsh treatment they receive, God's sheep are still God's sheep. He will never forget or abandon them. Nor will He disown them, for they are precious in His sight.

Christ confirmed the shepherd's commitment to His sheep in the strongest terms. "My sheep hear My voice, and I know them, and they follow Me; and I give eternal life to them, and they shall never perish; and no one shall snatch them out of My hand. My Father, who has given them to Me, is greater than all; and no one is able to snatch them out of the Father's hand" (John 10:27–29). The security of the sheep is the Father and Son's highest priority.

Just imagine a shepherd who has been given, say, a hundred sheep in the morning and returns with ninety-four in the evening! He'd be ridiculed to his face for losing sheep entrusted to his care. He might protest that the sheep were stubborn, or that they followed false paths and did not want to be brought back into the sheepfold. Even so, his reputation would be tarnished. Shepherds have full responsibility for sheep, no matter how irascible the sheep might be.

The sheep (that's those of us who believe on Christ) are a gift from the Father to the Son. We are in the Son's hands and in the hands of the Father too. Here are two pairs of hands that work in harmony—a double security for sheep who are prone to wander.

If you are still unconvinced, protesting that "Christ holds onto the hands of His own, but we can—if we wrest our hands away from Him—slip through His fingers," I reply that the matter is not quite that simple. We are one of His fingers (Ephesians 5:30)!

Believers have lined up with God's purposes. They have the assurance that if they have personally trusted the Shepherd, they are secure from here to eternity. God won't forsake them even in their rebellion.

This morning a note was on my desk telling of a born-again Christian who committed suicide. He walked outside and shot himself, leaving behind a grieving wife and shocked children. The reasons are unclear, except that He was weary of the emotional pain he suffered when he was abused as a child. Though he loved Christ, he thought he just couldn't take it anymore.

Of course no one knows the heart of a person except God. But I'm convinced that those who have trusted Christ are in heaven today even if they die with the sin of murder on their conscience. Even rebellious sheep are taken from earth to heaven.

The Son will not lose those whom the Father has entrusted to Him.

Children of the heav'nly Father
Safely in His bosom gather;
Nestling bird nor star in heaven
Such a refuge ne'er was given.

Neither life nor death shall ever
From the Lord His children sever;
Unto them His grace He showeth,
And their sorrows all He knoweth.

GOD, TED TURNER, AND YOU

But what do we make of Ted Turner, who said he was saved seven or eight times but felt better when he lost his faith? What do we make of all those who turn away from the truth they once knew? These are difficult questions, and we must treat them carefully, for only God sees the human heart.

Of course, the fact that God has a place reserved for us in heaven could lead some to misuse this assurance. But the new birth gives us a love for God, a desire to live for Him rather than ourselves. Our motivation is to be a servant of Christ, not a servant of the Devil.

Suppose a young woman becomes engaged to a man. She knows that he is trustworthy. He will keep his word to marry her. Does she then use this promise as an excuse to sleep with other men, knowing that her fiancé will marry her no matter what? Of course not! She loves her suitor. His commitment to marry her makes her love him more. Secure in his love, she wants to please him in everything.

Just so, those whom God has reconciled to Himself desire to please Him. Realistically, we have to admit that grace can be misused; yes, even abused. A true believer may actually turn from the faith; and if so, the Father will discipline His child for disobedience. Indeed, such discipline is proof of sonship (see Hebrews 12:6–8). That discipline might not always be effective, for sometimes God's children can be stubborn, but it will be administered. God won't abandon His children who misbehave.

But—and this is important—we also have to remember that many people who think they have trusted Christ as their Savior have not. They might never have been one of God's sheep, though they have heard about the Shepherd all of their lives and know some of His sheep. Later, they turn away from something they never really had; they deny a faith they only thought was theirs.

Let's listen as Ted Turner continues to explain his understanding of why he rejects the work of Christ for himself.

If you really accept the Bible for what it says, the New Testament at any rate, the way it is generally interpreted, then everyone is going to hell. This idea of sin is horrible and disgusting. Christ had to come down here and suffer and die on the cross so that with his blood our sins could be washed away . . . weird man! I'm telling you! Nobody has to die on the cross and have a blood sacrifice the way these ancient religions did down here in the pyramids of Mexico where they cut out virgins' hearts.[2]

Just a couple of observations. First, Turner obviously believes that a blood sacrifice is not necessary to take away sins. But whether such a sacrifice is needed is not really for us to decide. If the Bible is a reliable revelation from God, as all the evidence attests, then whether Christ had to die on the cross to save us from our sins is not really our call. We don't make the rules by which God operates.

Second, to equate the sacrifice of Christ to the cutting out of the hearts of virgins in pagan religions is to turn away blindly from the chasm that exists between Christ and other religious teachers and beliefs. There is an infinite difference between Christianity, which demands a divine-human sacrifice, and paganism, where sinners kill other sinners in a futile attempt to take away their sins. Even pagans know that a sacrifice is needed to take away sins, but Christianity alone gives the reason that the sacrifice of Christ is the only one that God accepts.

Turner's words are those of a man who has never understood the basics of the Christian faith. He might have prayed prayers, heard the gospel, even made a decision, but the seed of God's Word never took root in his heart. He must have thought that one becomes a Christian by trying to live a Christian life. When that led nowhere, as well it might, he jettisoned "faith." The Bible is filled with warnings to apostates who turn away from the faith they claim to have once embraced.

In Canada a crew of men sold evergreens to a neighborhood and then showed up to plant them. Despite repeated watering, the small trees began to wither, stubbornly refusing to grow. Exasperated, one resident dug up one of the trees and discovered he could have pulled it out of the ground with one hand. These men, frauds that they were, had just taken evergreen branches and stuck them in the ground!

Christ has a word for the Ted Turners of this world. When the Pharisees were offended by some of the harsh remarks He made to them, He answered simply, "Every plant which My heavenly Father did not plant shall be rooted up" (Matthew 15:13). If we have not been "planted by God," our commitment to Christ is not only shallow, but a mirage. The decisions we make pass away; what God does abides. In this life, the wheat and the tares grow up together, sometimes indistinguishable from one another. But at the time of the harvest, they shall be separated. God knows those who are His.

What kind of faith saves?

Bishop Munsey tells a parable of a man who, while walking along, suddenly fell off the edge of a cliff. As he hurtled down, he was able to reach out and grab a limb jutting out of the rock. He grasped it and hung suspended over the jagged rocks below.

The story goes that an angel appeared, and the man pleaded for the angel to save him. The angel responded, "Do you believe that I *can* save you?" The man saw the strong arms of the angel and said, "Yes, I believe that you are able to save me!"

The angel then asked, "Do you believe that I *will* save you?" The man saw the smile on the angel's face and replied, "Yes, I believe you will save me!"

Then the angel said, "If you believe that I can save you and if you believe that I will save you, *let go!*"

That "letting go" is faith. We quit clinging to our baptism, our good deeds, our own efforts to please God. We turn from our own sinfulness and transfer our trust to Christ. When we rely on Him to save us, He does. "Truly, truly, I say to you, he who hears My word, and believes Him who sent Me, has eternal life, and does not come into judgment, but has passed out of death into life" (John 5:24). That's a promise you can count on.

We've learned that there are many people who have not believed on Christ but only *think* they have, and that there are also many who have believed but are not sure of it. They wonder: Have I *really* believed?

On what does assurance rest? How do we really know that we will spend eternity with God?

These questions will be discussed in the next chapter.

NOTES

1. Ted Turner, in *The Humanist,* January/February 1991, 13.
2. Ibid.

CHAPTER SIX

*S*AVED
FOR SURE

In Michelangelo's painting of the final judgment, the expressions on the faces of those who are about to be judged reflect uncertainty and fear. No one in the fresco except the Virgin Mary knows his or her fate.

What expression would be on our faces if we knew that, say, in exactly one hour, we would be face-to-face with God? Samuel Johnson observed, "Nothing focuses the mind like the knowledge that one is to be hanged!" No matter how much confidence we profess, we all have our apprehensions about crossing the boundary into the unknown.

Yet, despite our anxieties, we can have a settled conviction that God will accept us without hesitation or reservation. He does not play games with us, keeping us off-balance, spiritually speaking. A loving Father would want His children to know that they belong to Him. Death, though mysterious, need not terrify us.

Here is a promise we can claim: "Since then the children share in flesh and blood, He Himself likewise also partook of the same, that through death He might render powerless him who had the power of death, that is, the Devil; and might deliver those who through fear of death were subject to slavery all their lives" (Hebrews 2:14–15). Christ came to free us from the terrors of death!

Paul compares death to the sting of a bee. "O death, where is your victory? O death, where is your sting?" (1 Corinthians 15:55). After a bee has stung its victim, it cannot sting again, regardless of how menacing its sound as it approaches a bare arm. Just so, death exhausted itself in Christ. Its sting has been removed. It can only frighten, not destroy.

In the previous chapter I gave reasons for God's bringing His children safely home. But now we come to the crucial question: How can we have the assurance that we are one of God's children? It is wonderful to believe that those who are saved are secure forever, but the pressing question now is *How can we know that we're included in that special number?*

We'll identify true faith more easily after we have contrasted it with some counterfeits. Just stay with me.

A FAITH THAT WILL NOT SAVE

When Paul wrote to the church at Corinth he reminded them that he always determined to know nothing among them "except Jesus Christ and Him crucified." He did this, he said, "that your faith should not rest on the wisdom of men, but on the power of God" (1 Corinthians 2:5). He feared lest their faith was on a wrong foundation.

The characteristics of true faith will become clearer if we contrast it with some popular notions that fall short of a faith that actually saves. The difference is between the wisdom of men and the power of God.

First, there is the "I believe in Christ and . . ." kind of faith. Mutual funds, as you know, spread the risk of your financial investment. Your money purchases shares in a number of different companies so that if one goes bankrupt the others will make up for it, and in the end your investment will be safe.

That's the way some people think of their faith in Christ. They believe in Him, but they also believe that baptism helps to save them, as do the Eucharist, church attendance, and good works. If one of those doesn't get them into heaven, another will. Or, perhaps when added together, all those will accumulate enough merit to lead one to God.

In a restaurant, a woman stopped to greet a friend of mine, and we struck up a conversation about religion in general and Christianity in particular. In the course of the discussion I asked her, "Why do you think God will let you into heaven?"

She replied, "My husband and I earned twelve hundred dollars in a bake sale, which we gave to charity." When I asked whether she had anything else to offer God, she mentioned a number of other good things she had done.

"And what if God demands more?" I persisted. She replied that she would depend on the grace of God for the rest.

At this point our mutual friend told this story:

A man came to the pearly gates of heaven and was asked by Saint Peter why he should be admitted into heaven.

The man replied, "My parents had me baptized."

Peter replied, "That's worth five points."

"I went to church every week."

"That's worth twenty points."

"I went to confession twice a year."

"That's worth ten points."

"I had an honest business"

"That's five points."

With this, the man became fearful, for he could think of no other merit he had accumulated. Simple arithmetic told him that he had only forty of the one hundred points needed. But, fortunately, he remembered a sermon he had heard on grace, so he answered, "I'm depending on the grace of God."

To which Peter replied, "You are lucky—the grace of God is worth sixty points!"

Of course a theologian might want to correct the story a bit and say that even the other forty points were God's grace, since He gives us the strength to do good deeds. Even so, in the story salvation is seen as a cooperative effort between man and God. It is based on the supposition that we can contribute toward the miracle we so desperately need.

As politely as possible, I tried to help this dear woman realize that those who distribute their faith between Christ and other works and rituals insult Him. They have not yet grasped that Christ alone is qualified to make us acceptable to God. They are like the Pharisee who trusted in God *and* in himself for salvation. For that error he left the temple without having been justified.

When I asked the woman if she was *sure* that she had done enough to enter heaven, she had to confess that, no, she was not sure that she would make it. And with good reason. Because she thinks salvation is partly of God's grace and partly of her own deeds, she can never be certain that she has lived up to her part of the bargain.

I challenged her to go for broke. I told her that there was a faith that could actually save her. It was the kind of faith that would lead to assurance and could take her safely all the way to heaven. More about that later.

Then there is the "I believe in Christ in a general sense . . ." kind of faith. Such a person might even believe that Christ died for sinners, but he or she does not accept this gift personally. There can be a change of mind without a conviction within the heart.

Just as deceptive is an "I went forward in a meeting and prayed a prayer . . ." kind of faith. This faith confuses an outward sign with an inward miracle. I've already warned about the dangers of associating genuine salvation with walking forward in a meeting or signing a decision card. When I was about ten years old I was too shy to walk in front of several hundred people while an invitation hymn was being sung. So I suffered through those moments thinking I could never be saved. I was thinking, *If I have to go forward to be saved, I guess I'll just go to hell!*

Somehow we just don't think God has done anything in our hearts until we have contributed to it. We want to at least raise our hand, walk down an aisle, or perform some other religious ritual. Those who confuse faith in Christ with such routines often backslide—and with good reason! They think they are saved because they have done something! And yet the transfer of trust might not have been made.

If you are inclined to believe that your own performance helps purchase your salvation, I have a question for you: *What makes you think that your good works could possibly mean more to God than the merits of His Son, whom He so deeply loves?* The good news is that Christ died saying, "It is finished." That expression really means "Paid in full."

To grasp this comes to the heart of a faith that saves.

THE FAITH THAT SAVES

The faith that saves is based on a conviction, a settled belief in some facts. "Now faith is the assurance of things hoped for, the conviction of things not seen" (Hebrews 11:1). That word *assurance* can also mean confidence. Faith, then, is a *conviction,* a sense of assurance that something is true. And if we are convinced of the right things, we will be saved.

Notice how the apostle John connects the assurance of salvation with an inner witness or conviction within the heart:

> If we receive the witness of men, the witness of God is greater; for the witness of God is this, that He has borne witness concerning His Son. The one who believes in the Son of God has the witness in himself; the one who does not believe God has made Him a liar, because he has not believed in the witness that God has borne concerning His Son. And the witness is this, that God has given us eternal life, and this life is in His Son. He who has the Son has the life; he who does not have the Son of God does not have the life. These things I have written to you who believe in the name of the Son of God, in order that you may know that you have eternal life. (1 John 5:9–13)

What are the characteristics of saving faith? What kind of faith gives us such assurance that we "know we have eternal life"?

A Faith Directed to Christ Alone

Saving faith means that I accept Christ as my substitute, my sin-bearer. I cherish and believe Christ's promises that He will give eternal life to those who believe. Calvin defined it as "the firm and certain knowledge of God's benevolence toward us, founded upon the truth of the freely given promise of Christ, both revealed to our minds and sealed upon our hearts by the Holy Spirit."[1] This is a faith that is given to us by God, an understanding that Christ did all that is necessary to declare us forever righteous before God.

The faith that saves is a personal affirmation of belief. The apostle Paul put it this way: "If you confess with your mouth Jesus as Lord, and believe in your heart that God raised Him from the dead, you shall be saved; for with the heart man believes, resulting in righteousness, and with the mouth he confesses, resulting in salvation. For the Scripture says, 'Whoever believes in Him will not be disappointed'" (Romans 10:9–10). This is a trust of the heart, not just the nodding approval of the mind.

R. T. Kendall correctly writes, "We are saved because we are persuaded that Jesus Christ is the Son of God, the God-man, and that He paid our debt by His shed blood on the cross. . . . If we are not persuaded that Christ has paid our debt there can be no assurance of saving faith, hence no assurance of salvation."[2]

Don't miss this: We must believe that Christ did all that is necessary and ever will be necessary for us to stand in the sight of God. If we have such faith, we will have assurance; we will know that we have eternal life.

Obviously, the more deeply we believe that Christ did all that is necessary for us, the greater our assurance. We might begin with a small faith (Christ said that faith the size of a mustard seed was all that is required), and within time it will grow.

Whether our faith be little or much, it must be directed to Christ *alone,* for God accepts only those who accept His Son. And the more surely we are persuaded that His merit was completely accepted by God the Father, the more confident we will be that we are saved, and saved forever.

No wonder the figures in Michelangelo's painting of final judgment have consternation on their faces! In medieval times, the people, for the most part, were not taught that Christ paid the full debt of sin for all who believe. They were told that salvation was a cooperative effort between man and God. Churchgoers were discouraged from thinking that salvation was a gift; rather, they were expected to merit the merit of Christ. They had to add to His work through their own works and sufferings. Obviously, with that kind of theology, no one was ever sure that he had done enough. Those who said they had assurance were accused of being presumptuous.

Contrast this with Charles Spurgeon, a preacher in London in the last century, who is quoted as saying that he could swing above the flames of hell hanging on to a flax stalk and not fear damnation, provided he was trusting Christ alone for his salvation! That's not presumption—it is simply believing the promises of Christ no matter what. The difference is whether Christ did it all or we must help Him out.

Salvation is a matter of trusting a qualified Savior. It embraces Christ's work as sufficient. It transfers confidence from ourselves to Someone who actually has the credentials to meet God's high standard. Even better, it is a faith that believes that God's standard has already been met for those who believe. By Christ's death we are reconciled to God; by His resurrection we are assured that His sacrifice for us was accepted. For those who believe, it's a done deal!

Suppose someone says, "I can't be a Christian because I can't live the Christian lifestyle." Such a person still has not understood the good news. We do not have to live a Christian life in order to help Christ save us. He does the changing; He does whatever is needed to fit us for heaven above and to live on the earth below. He does not expect us to change ourselves first. He requires only that we see our sinfulness and our need for Christ's righteousness.

When at the age of fourteen I realized that I did not have to walk forward in a meeting to be saved, I accepted Christ personally; I understood Him to be my sin-bearer. From that moment I have had the settled conviction that I am saved—and saved forever. I learned that God can work anywhere and at any time. To be saved is not just something we decide to do (though it is a decision); nor is it merely the assent of the mind (though it is that too). True faith is a persuasion of the heart. It is a conviction that is wrought within us by the Holy Spirit. It is nothing less than a gift of God.

Let me say it once more: *If you are persuaded that Christ did all that is necessary and all that ever will be necessary to bring you to God, you not only will be saved, but* know it!

Today you and I should be able to say with Paul, "For this reason I also suffer these things, but I am not ashamed; for I know whom I have believed and I am convinced that He is able to guard what I have entrusted to Him until that day" (1 Timothy 1:12). If we were to ask Paul where this deep conviction originated, he would reply, "Faith comes from hearing, and hearing by the word of Christ" (Romans 10:17).

If you, my friend, are convinced in your heart that Christ paid your debt, and you are resting your eternal soul on Christ and nothing else, you too are saved—and saved forever. That is good news in a day of depressing headlines and an uncertain economy.

A Faith Confirmed by the Holy Spirit

The new birth, as we have learned, is not something we do but something that God does in us. We receive a new nature, but also the Holy Spirit takes up residence within us.

Listen to the words of Paul: "The Spirit Himself bears witness with our spirit that we are children of God, and if children, heirs also, heirs of God and fellow heirs with Christ, if indeed we suffer with Him in order that we may also be glorified with Him" (Romans 8:16–17). The Spirit gives us an inner witness that we are indeed children of God. There is a sense of "belongingness," an inner conviction that, at long last, we have been reconciled to God. We begin to think of ourselves differently, for we are under new management.

God works directly in the hearts of those who are His. He does not do this through means of grace that are carried out by men, but He works in combination with the faith that has been planted within the heart. The church does not have the power to include or to exclude men from God's grace.

We can't repeat too often that salvation is God's work. We are saved directly by God and not by men acting in His behalf. The sacraments are symbols of what God does, but in themselves they are not the means of salvation. A soul can be saved without baptism, the Eucharist, and other rituals. In fact, a soul is saved *only apart from the rituals that men can perform.*

That explains why John can say, "The one who believes in the Son of God has the witness in himself" (1 John 5:10). The church cannot do this for us; God does this particular work quite apart from His ministers. If you believe that Christ paid your debt for both now and forever, you will have this inner witness that you are God's child.

We can all learn a lesson from John Wesley, an English eighteenth-century evangelist who came to America to convert the Indians. But he returned to England with an overwhelming conviction that he had a sinful heart that had never been reborn. He wrote, "I have learned what I least of all suspected, that I, who went to America to convert the Indians, was never myself converted to God!"

Wesley envied the faith of his friends, who spoke of their confidence that they had come to know God, a faith that brought joy and peace. Wesley would have given his last drop of blood to have that kind of faith for himself. When he was told that it was a gift given to those who wanted it, he determined he would seek it.

On May 24, 1738, he quite unwillingly attended a meeting on Aldersgate Street, where a man was reading aloud from Luther's preface to the book of Romans. Wesley writes, "About a quarter before nine, while he was describing the change which God works in the heart through faith in Christ, I felt my heart strangely warmed. I felt that I did trust in Christ, Christ alone for my salvation: And an assurance was given me that He had taken away my sins, even mine, and saved me from the law of sin and death."

That is how personal faith in Christ must become to have the assurance that the miracle of the new birth has happened within us. Once such trust was in Wesley's heart, the assurance was there too. Notice the words, "I felt I did trust Christ, Christ alone. . . . And an assurance was given me that He had taken away my sins, even mine . . ."

Trust in Christ alone saves. That trust, thanks to the power of the Holy Spirit, leads to assurance.

A Faith That Bears Spiritual Fruit

I have gone to great lengths to show that we are not saved by good works but that, once we are saved by Christ's grace, we are expected to live a life of good works (see Ephesians 2:10). The inner transformation of life wrought by the Holy Spirit brings about fruit in the life of a Christian.

117

Our works are now pleasing to God because we as individuals have been made pleasing to God through the perfect merits of Christ. The works we did before we were justified were worthless, even a stumbling block, in our quest for God. The works that follow justification are made acceptable to God because we are now His children and serve Him with love and gratitude. Christ now makes our imperfect works perfect in God's sight.

After our conversion, we see God differently. Rather than thinking of him as an impersonal, distant being, we will now speak to Him as a heavenly Father. We will also see sin differently. Rather than something to be tolerated and perhaps even enjoyed, we now see it as something that offends God.

What role do good works play in our assurance of salvation? They confirm our decision, but they cannot become the basis of our assurance. They provide a secondary kind of test, either encouraging us to gain a stronger assurance or, conversely, if there is no change of heart, giving us good reason to question our salvation. But personal assurance is first and foremost rooted in our faith in Christ.

If someone tells me that he has accepted Christ as his Savior yet lives the same selfish, sin-oriented life as before, I have reason to think that he might just be self-deceived. After all, as this book has shown, the work of God in the heart is deep and lasting. Not only should we question someone's salvation if his life is unchanged, but he should question it too.

On the other hand, if someone's faith has borne fruit, if there has been a transformation of life, then we have reason to think that his faith in Christ might be genuine. We can encourage him but should stop short of pronouncing him "saved."

We need to trust the Holy Spirit to give him the conviction that leads to assurance. Because we cannot see what is in the human heart, we can only point the way, but we cannot tell a person he has arrived. Remember: Many churchgoers who claim to be Christians aren't, though they think they are.

Until he was thirty-four, a friend of mine, reared in an evangelical church, believed he was a Christian. Others also thought of him as a fine Christian, the kind of person whose presence changed the attitude of those around him. People stopped their swearing when he walked into the room; no shady deals were concocted within his hearing. And yet, through a series of circumstances, he was led to deep conviction of sin and later was converted. I was interested to hear him say, "I didn't know that I was unsaved until the morning I got saved!"

I cannot impart assurance to you, nor can I judge you if you tell me that you have been persuaded in your heart that Christ has taken your penalty of sin away. If you doubt, I can counsel you to look at Christ, study His perfect works, and lay hold of His marvelous promises.

As a pastor I have counseled those who seek God but lack assurance of their salvation. One man read his Bible a few hours each day trying to gain assurance. Another went on a retreat to "seek God." As long as these men looked to their works, they never thought they had enough to "prove" they were saved. In both cases I had every reason to believe that they were indeed born again. (Who else would be so concerned about assurance except someone in whose life God had already done a great work?) But my responsibility was not to impart assurance but to counsel them to look to Christ and embrace His completed work for themselves.

Obviously, if we look to our works, we will never have enough by which we can say, "I now know for sure that I am saved, now and forever." Furthermore, we can't be sure that the good works will continue in the future. Some Christians have walked away from God for years, giving little outward evidence of conversion.

Suppose you were on a plane and asked a fellow passenger, "Why should God accept you into heaven?" and he were to reply, "Because I am a good person, I give money to charity and do volunteer work in a hospital, and live an honest life." You would, I hope, have every reason to doubt whether he was indeed a Christian, for as we have been at pains to prove, no one is ever saved by good works.

If it is idolatry to try to be saved by good works, it most assuredly is misleading to say that our primary basis of assurance is good works! To quote Calvin once more, "If men begin to judge whether they are regenerate by good works nothing will ever be more uncertain or more evil."[3] When we look at ourselves, we have only reason to despair. It is impossible to derive perfect assurance from our imperfect works. We are saved by looking to Christ's "good works" and not our own. Thanks to Him, we can have the inner certainty that He has stood in our place and paid our debt.

A new convert can have assurance if he is convinced that Christ bore his sin and did all that needs to be done on his behalf. Such a faith will be confirmed by the inner witness of the Spirit. The new convert's future works (or lack of them) can challenge the genuineness of his faith, but if he has believed God's promises for himself, he can even now rest in their certainty. The hymn is right:

The vilest offender who truly believes,
That moment from Jesus a pardon receives.

His faith should not be in the evidence for faith but in the promise of Christ.

Doubts must be taken seriously, and doubt must be resolved biblically. Remember, there are people who do not believe the gospel but just think they do. And there are those who think they do not believe the gospel but actually do!

More about that in the next chapter.

A Faith That Grows

A couple at a conference asked me to give my counsel to the wife, who had occasional bouts of fear that she was not a Christian. Meanwhile, she had led Bible studies, had introduced others to faith in Christ, and gave every indication that she was indeed born again. I told her a story that helped her understand how our faith can grow.

There was a man, the story goes, who wanted to cross a small lake in winter but feared that the ice could not hold him. To make it less likely that he would fall through, he distributed his weight by crawling, rather than walking, on top of the ice. Suddenly he looked up and saw a team of horses coming toward him on the lake! With that, he stood up and began to walk on the ice with confidence.

"That's what I'm doing!" this doubting woman said. "I am crawling on the ice while others have the confidence to walk or even skate!" To which I replied, "Yes, and remember: The ice under your feet is just as thick as it is under the rest of us!" She was encouraged to stand up and walk, spiritually speaking; she needed to know that Christ was just as strong for her as He is for anyone else.

To quote that old cliché, "We might tremble on the rock, but the rock beneath us never trembles!" The faith by which we receive Christ might be hesitant and trembling. But the amount of faith is not as important as the object of faith. We can come to Christ with our doubts and with our misgivings, and He will help us. We come believing that He is our only hope; we come trusting His promise to accept us.

We do not have to have a perfect faith to receive Christ. As we grow in our faith we will come to what the author of Hebrews calls a "full assurance of faith" (10:22); that is, we will grow in our confidence and ability to trust God. With the study of the Bible and strength that comes from fellowship with God's people, we will continue our pilgrimage en route to the heavenly city with a growing certainty.

Some who crawl today will walk tomorrow.

IS CHRIST ENOUGH?

While sitting in my study at the Moody Church, I received a phone call from a woman who was weeping, insisting that she speak with me.

Here is her story. She lived in a nursing home in Chicago, and each morning the Christian women there would sit together to listen to Christian radio. That particular morning they heard a message in which the minister stressed that assurance of salvation was based on good works. He stated that a true Christian might backslide once or twice but that he would always return in fellowship with Christ. Without these evidences, there could be no assurance. Salvation comes by looking to Christ, the minister said, but after that our assurance comes by "checking our fruit."

The woman wept as she told me that, although she had accepted Christ as her Savior at the age of nineteen and had even led her daughter to faith in Christ, she now felt that the preacher had told her that she was unsaved.

"Why do you say this?" I asked.

"Well, according to him, if you backslide more than three times, you are not a Christian. My Lord knows how many times I have failed Him! I backslid many times! The preacher gave the impression that unless you are almost perfect, you are not saved!"

"What are you trusting for your salvation?" I asked.

"Well, the blood of Christ—there is nothing else." Then she added, "I cannot take steel wool to my heart and scrub it—I must trust the blood of Christ."

"The blood of Christ is *enough,*" I told her.

"Are you sure?"

"Yes. I'm sure!"

By now she had stopped her weeping. I prayed with her on the telephone, and later she said, "As soon as I hang up, I'm going to tell the other women here in the room that the blood of Christ is enough!"

The book of Exodus records the clash of the Israelites and Pharaoh, who would not let them leave Egypt. God commanded Moses, you will recall, to tell the Israelites to put blood on the doorposts of their houses on the night of the Passover to keep the angel of death from entering their homes. I can imagine a frightened firstborn child asking his father, "Are you sure we will be safe?" The father could take him outside and show him the blood. "Yes, we will be safe."

In another home, a firstborn son might have been a notorious sinner. He might have been worse than one of the Egyptian sons who lived across the street. But there was no need to argue whose sin was greater. It was the blood on the doorpost that mattered.

Another firstborn might have been emotionally troubled with indecision and doubt. A skeptic might have knocked on the door, taunting him, reminding him that the houses of the Egyptians and the houses of the Israelites looked very much alike. If judgment came to one it would come to the other.

But the son of the Israelite need not have argued about the matter. All that he needed to do was to point to the blood on the door and remind his accuser that God had promised, "When I see the blood I will pass over you" (Exodus 12:13). In every case, it was not the extent of the sin, the shape of the house, or the emotional stability of the inhabitants that mattered. The difference was the blood.

Blessed are those who are confident that the blood of Christ, the sacrifice He made for sinners on the cross, is enough! To grasp that promise is to receive assurance.

If God is satisfied with the death of Christ, we should be too. And when we are, we no longer owe God any righteousness. The song has it right:

> *I need no other argument,*
> *I need no other plea,*
> *It is enough that Jesus died,*
> *And that He died for me.*

Such assurance produces a spirit of repentance—a willingness to turn from ourselves and our sins to Christ, whom we now love. Our lives are changed because the chasm between us and God has been bridged.

We are saved and saved forever.

And yet if you doubt, the next chapter is for you!

NOTES

1. John Calvin, *The Institutes of the Christian Religion*, ed. Tony Lane and Hilary Osborne (Grand Rapids: Baker, 1987), 144.

2. R. T. Kendall, "The Ground of Assurance," *Westminster Record,* Winter 1988, 26.

3. John Calvin, quoted in R. T. Kendall, "The Ground of Assurance," 29.

$\mathcal{F}$OR DOUBTERS ONLY

God moves in a mysterious way
His wonders to perform;
He plants His footsteps in the sea,
And rides upon the storm.

T hese words of William Cowper are widely
known. What is not so widely known is that the evening
he composed this poem, he tried to commit suicide. Although he wrote many poems that extolled the goodness
and mercy of God, he believed that he himself was
damned.

Cowper's mother died when he was six, and he was
sent away to a boarding school. Early in life he felt the
sting of rejection, the feeling that he was worthless, fit
only to be rejected by God and men. No one craved
God's acceptance as much as he; no one was more convinced that he would never experience it.

His first suicide attempt occurred in his thirties. He tried to drink laudanum, an opium solution he thought would put him into permanent sleep, but in the end, he could not bring himself to drink it. Later, he tried to commit suicide by cutting himself with a pen knife—which broke. Next he tried to hang himself, but the garter snapped and he slumped onto the floor. He wrote of that incident, "Though I had failed in my design, yet I had all the guilt of that to answer for; a sense of God's wrath and a deep despair of escaping it."

Cowper was convinced that he had committed the unpardonable sin. In his despair he wrote a poem titled "Lines Written During a Period of Insanity." He judged himself to be "damn'd below Judas." He described periods of horrible darkness, pain, and wild, incoherent thoughts. His sense of sin and expectation of punishment were overwhelming.

He was taken to live in a house for lunatics, where he suffered from terrible visions and voices. Through wise counsel, he improved somewhat and even planned to marry. But later he suffered his second attack of full-blown insanity.

John Newton, the author of the hymn "Amazing Grace," invited Cowper into his home. There, Cowper—now suffering from paranoia—believed his food was poisoned. Again he tried suicide, thinking he heard God's voice condemning him to eternal punishment for his past failures in trying to end his life. He wrote about God's grace, yet believed that he himself was excluded from it.

Newton tried to reason Cowper out of his despair, but to no avail. Yet, though his battles with depression grew even more intense, Cowper continued to write poetry, extolling the wonders of the gospel. He wrote ballads for use in William Wilberforce's campaign against slavery, and he honored God's sovereignty over the affairs of men.

Finally, after another bout with insanity, he wrote no more hymns. Though he believed he was damned by God by a providential decree, he clung to the hope that God might one day relent and change His mind. His last six years were spent haunted by horrific dreams at night and depression during the day. He died believing he was doomed to hell.

We wish this story had a happy ending. It would have been wonderful indeed if Cowper had come to peaceful assurance just prior to his death. We could wish he had experienced the peace he longed for. He did not. He who understood God's grace wavered as he grasped for it himself.[1]

Cowper's friends had no doubt that he was a Christian, primarily because of his steadfast perseverance, honesty, and deep desire to do God's will, whatever the cost. In other words, this was an instance in which good works testified to saving grace, and it is an example of how we can see the work of God in the life of a believer, even if he or she cannot.

Who but a person in whom God did a mighty work would so passionately desire to be included in the circle of God's mercy? Who but a believer would write about the grace of God, even when he felt he was not included in the circle of those who were blessed? Who but a believer would defend God's right to judge men, even when he thought that he himself would be the object of such judgment?

Of course we cannot be sure, for only God knows the human heart. But it is certainly possible that Cowper was a believer, for as we have seen elsewhere in this book, there are many people who are saved but lack personal assurance.

There is no despair so deep, no depression so dark, as the belief that one cannot, for whatever reason, be saved.

It is my hope that by the time you have finished reading this chapter, you will be saved and *know* it. And if you already know it, I pray that your assurance will be greater still.

A man faced heart surgery with confidence, believing that he would make it through the operation successfully. Yet he fretted the night before, fearful of what would happen when he went under the doctor's knife.

"I thought you were sure that everything will be all right," his wife tried to reassure him.

"I am sure that everything will be all right," he replied. "But it's just that I'm not *sure* that I'm *sure!*"

Yes, we might be sure that we will go to heaven when we die. But being sure that we are sure is the problem!

We have said earlier that some people who doubt their salvation should do so. They have good reason to be unsure: they have never had the faith that saves. For them, doubt is helpful, for it might lead them to examine their faith. Doubt, if properly used, can be the servant of truth. Of course, the perpetual doubt of the skeptic who holds Christ at arms' length leads to damnation. But the doubt of the honest seeker can lead to assurance. We must analyze our doubts and learn from them.

REASONS FOR DOUBT

Why do some true believers doubt?

Uncertainty Regarding the
Time of Their Conversion

Most Christians can give the day and the hour when they came to saving faith in Christ. Others, particularly those who were brought up in Christian homes, may have had personal faith in Christ at such an early age that they do not remember when they crossed the line and were "born again."

"I'm not saved, but my parents tell me that I am!" the young woman said to me. "I don't even remember when I accepted Christ as my Savior." She needed this bit of counsel: It is possible to know that the sun is shining even if we do not know the time of the sunrise!

The question is not whether we can remember the day or the hour in the past, but whether our faith is in Christ in the present. Are we now persuaded that Christ met all of our obligations for us when He died on the cross? And if not, rather than analyze the past, why not accept Christ as our personal sin-bearer now? We cannot revisit the past, but we can acknowledge our faith in Christ in the present.

Contributing to this lack of assurance is the teaching that we must "accept Jesus into our hearts," an expression that is not found in the Bible. I just read an account of someone who "accepted Christ as his Savior" three times a year! I, for one, prayed a prayer to "accept Jesus" every night for months when I was a child and yet lacked assurance. Every evening before I went to bed, I prayed the prayer again, but in my mind nothing happened. I thought myself doomed.

Some questions we should ask are: Why do we have to "accept Jesus into our heart"? What difference will He make when this happens? How will having Jesus in our heart rectify our relationship with God? How will we know it has happened? The expression is confusing.

The gospel is not primarily Christ in my heart (although it is that) but Christ as my *sin-bearer.* It was when I understood that Christ had died for me and must be received by faith, not feelings, that I had the assurance that I had been accepted by God. When we speak of Christ as the One who died and took our penalty, then faith has an objective basis.

Faulty Teaching

If you were taught that the possibility that you will be saved tomorrow does not exist until tomorrow comes; if you believe that you can lose your salvation whenever you cease to believe or fall into sin, then assurance is beyond reach.

That is why I tried to establish in an earlier chapter the doctrine of the security of the believer. If we are not sure that our relationship with God is eternally secure, it is very difficult to grow in the Christian life. We must have the confidence that if we have truly believed, we shall not be lost.

The Power of Guilt

I receive many letters from people who think they have committed the unpardonable sin. A small voice seems to say to them, "If you were a Christian you would not have done that . . . you would not have behaved this way!"

These doubters must remember that it is possible for Christians to do terrible things. When this happens, God does discipline those who are His, but He does not cast them off. In fact, their own sense of guilt might play a part in God's discipline in restoring them to fellowship with God.

Guilt is used by God only until his children repent. After that there is false guilt, which is exploited by Satan, the "accuser of the brethren." He enjoys engendering doubt in believers.

C. S. Lewis, in *The Screwtape Letters,* has the senior demon give instructions to his nephew about how to cause Christians to lose their confidence in God. He says the best way to do that is to get them to stop thinking about God and instead think about their state of mind. They must, at all costs, be preoccupied with their feelings and doubts; they must be made to wallow in uncertainties so that they will be discouraged.

As for the "unpardonable sin," it is committed only by unbelievers who harden their hearts against God. Those who seek God's forgiveness, no matter how great their sin, can be assured of mercy. That is why it is often said that those who are troubled about whether they have committed the unpardonable sin almost certainly have not done so.

Those who *have* committed this sin have seared their conscience and have no qualms about their rebellion. They have no desire to seek God for forgiveness. They probably would never read this book!

Confusion Between Faith and Feelings

Some people think that saving faith entails an instantaneous spiritual experience that will flood them with overwhelming peace and joy. Sometimes that does happen, but often it does not. We must remember that faith, not feelings, is the basis for our assurance.

Martin Luther was once asked if he felt saved. He replied, "No I don't feel saved, but my confidence in Christ's promise is greater than my doubts!" And that, at the end of the day, is the basis of assurance—the belief that Christ was not lying to us when He said that we could believe on Him and be saved.

The Effect of Personal Rebellion

We have all met Christians who doubt because they have turned away from what they know to be right. Understandably, the Holy Spirit is grieved because of their sin, and peace from God eludes them. Recently I spoke to a homosexual who believes he accepted Christ at the age of twenty, only to plunge into a life of wanton immorality. He became so angry with God that he even asked

God to remove from his mind the verses of Scripture he had learned. For ten years he quenched the prompting of the Holy Spirit.

However, in recent months he has repented and has "come clean." He has left the homosexual lifestyle and speaks openly about God's deliverance from this "mountain of guilt," as he called it. He also tells of the wonderful joy of assurance—the knowledge that he belongs to God forever. That assurance was lost during his days of rebellion. Whether or not he was a child of God during those days of heedless carnality (who of us knows for sure?), he lost fellowship with his Father. Assurance comes to our hearts most strongly when our faith is living.

The Chronic Doubter

Finally, there are those who, like Cowper, have become chronic doubters. They wallow in introspection and find it practically impossible to look away from themselves to Christ. They are unable to grasp the wonder of God's grace and cannot see that what Christ did can be applied to them. For whatever reason, they see themselves as sinners too vile to save.

And yet they believe. They cling to Christ and throw themselves upon His mercy. They trust, but they are not persuaded; they hope, though they are not assured. The inner confidence eludes them. These are the William Cowpers of this world.

Why are they saved? Because they accept the premise that if they are to be saved at all, they will be saved by God's grace through Christ. Their faith wavers, but it is directed toward the right person. Whatever else might be said about Cowper, he was under no illusions that he could be saved through living a good life and cooperating with God in salvation. Much better to believe in grace with a trembling heart than to believe in works with steady confidence.

Such doubters also often give evidence of being saved because of an implanted desire to please Christ. Though they believe they have been rejected by God, their greatest longing is that He be honored. This is further evidence of the work of God within them. Just as Moses, who did not know that his face shone when he came down from the mountain, though the people did (Exodus 34:29–30), so we often see the life of Christ in the believer even when he or she does not. The marks of grace are often found in the lives of these troubled souls even while they lack the assurance of such grace.

These doubters must be contrasted with volitional doubters, those who choose to not believe. We have all met unbelievers who fold their hands over their chests, sit back in their chairs, assume an air of superiority, and confidently say, "I dare you to convince me!" They are closed to faith.

Cowper was not a volitional doubter. He did not choose to not believe. He longed to believe but felt he could not. Although he held to the grace of God with a trembling hand, I believe he grasped the treasure nevertheless. For such, there is mercy.

There is a great deal of difference between a weak faith and a wrong faith. We might not believe the truths of the gospel as firmly as, say, the apostle Peter did. Yet, as Luther pointed out,

> two persons may hold glasses of wine in their hands; the hand of one trembles, the other does not. Two persons may hold a purse full of money: one with a weak hand, the other with a strong hand. Whether the hand is strong or weak, it neither increases nor decreases the contents of the purse. So the only difference between me and St. Peter is that he holds the treasure more firmly.[2]

Even a weak faith saves if it is directed to Christ alone. But a wrong faith leads to destruction, even if it is held with unwavering confidence. Those who cling to their good deeds or to a false savior will be damned, no matter how strong their trust. It is, after all, Christ alone who saves.

HELP FOR DOUBTERS

Here are some principles that will help us personally to resolve our doubts or give us the direction we need to help others who struggle with assurance.

Identify the Cause of Doubt

If, as someone has said, it is true that "he who has never doubted has never believed," doubts must be considered as healthy if they prod us in the direction of faith.

Properly interpreted, doubt should lead to probing, questioning, and testing of ideas. Alister McGrath put it this way: Suppose you want to see the stars or catch a glimpse of the Milky Way. You can't do this in broad daylight. You have to wait until it is dark. The stars don't need darkness to exist, but we need darkness in order to see them. We can be told about the existence of the stars, but only in the night do we see them. Just so, it is often in the darkness that we see God.

It is interesting that those who have experienced the severest doubts often emerge with the strongest faith. We should, as much as possible, create an atmosphere where doubts can be openly expressed. Many a child raised in a Christian home has grown up with the notion that to doubt is to disbelieve, and to disbelieve is to be damned.

Obviously, God wants to bring us through our doubts to the light of assurance. But the starting point is to voice our doubts, to talk about the barriers that hinder us from belief.

Some people struggle with factual doubt. They question the reliability of the Bible and the basis for the Christian faith. These people need instruction in apologetics, the rationality of the Christian faith. Many books have been written that give a defense of Christianity over against other options. Of course, we cannot prove Christianity with mathematical certainty. If that were possible, there would be no need for faith. But we can give reasons that are powerful enough for an honest doubter, but not a dishonest one.

There is no formula for dealing with doubters. "We come into the world with question marks in our heads," someone has said. Each person comes with his own questions, apprehensions, and reasons not to believe. We cannot bring a person to faith in Christ, for only the Holy Spirit can do that. We can, however, clear away misconceptions, answer questions, and encourage people to give the gospel a hearing.

Doubts must be taken seriously. Remember that some people think they believe the gospel but don't; whereas others, like Cowper, might have doubts and yet do believe.

Magnify the Grace of God

For those who doubt because of the greatness of their sin or the fear that they are beyond God's mercy, we should not minimize their sin. Be thankful when people see their sins for what they are.

Those who are troubled by an oversensitive conscience often are told, "Your sin is not that bad—there are many people who have done things far worse than you." That may be true, and even be of small comfort, but the doubter is not impressed. He sees his sin as being a giant mountain, a barrier that is too great for God to overcome.

What do we say to a child molester who must daily live with the knowledge that he has ruined, perhaps permanently, the lives of others? Recently a man in prison for rape wrote to me, asking how he could be freed from the guilt of the past. I did not minimize his sin, but I did magnify grace! I explained why the only place to face such a burden of sin is in the presence of Jesus Christ. He is the friend of sinners.

On August 21, 1544, Martin Luther wrote a letter to one of his faithful and trusted co-workers, George Spalatin, who had given a friend some advice that he later regarded as sinful. Because of the harm he thought his suggestion would bring, Spalatin was immersed in grief and guilt. He would not be consoled.

Luther wrote to him. He did not minimize the sin but saw Christ as sufficient for great sinners.

> My faithful request and admonition is that you join our company and associate with us, who are real, great and hard-boiled sinners. You must by no means make Christ to seem paltry and trifling to us, as though He could be our Helper only when we want to be rid from imaginary, minimal and childish sins. No, no! That would not be good for us. He must rather be a Savior and Redeemer from real, great, grievous and damnable transgressions and iniquities, yea, from the very greatest and most shocking sins; to be brief, from all sins added together in a grand total. . . . You will have to get used to the belief that Christ is a real Savior and you a real sinner. For God is neither jesting nor dealing in imaginary affairs, but He was greatly and most assuredly in earnest when He sent His own Son into the world and sacrificed Him for our sakes.

Christ did not come to save only sinners who were reared in Christian homes, sinners whose greatest crime is to have angrily bent a golf club on a tree stump! No, He came to save big sinners, child molesters, rapists. Christ was not just a Savior for "respectable" sinners. He is a real Savior for real sinners.

Satan always wants us to see our sin as greater than God's grace. We must never forget that the grace that is in *God's* heart is greater than the sin that is in our past. God anticipated our sinfulness and is well able to clear the account of anyone who trusts His Son.

Teach the Fatherhood of God

Recently I spoke to a young man whose father was a strict disciplinarian, a man who was never pleased with his son's performance. Is it any wonder that this young man struggled with assurance, no matter how long and consistently he called on God? If the human love we experience is always conditional, if we have felt the deep hurt of rejection, we tend to think that God is just like the one who turned his back on us.

I am certainly not qualified to diagnose Cowper's spiritual struggles, but I would like to suggest that the root of his doubts originated in the rejection he felt as a child. Like many abused children, he felt helpless, unworthy of God's love and personal attention.

I have had more than one person tell me, "I had an earthly father who abused me. How can I trust my heavenly Father?" God wants to bring us through such times of doubt and develop confidence in Him despite our past.

We have to help people see that God is not like a man. Once He makes a promise to His people, He can be counted on to fulfill it. He does not delight in having children who are constantly doubting their paternity.

Cowper also wrestled with a theological problem that he did not correctly resolve. He grew up in an era when the doctrine of election was stressed, namely, the idea that God is the one who chooses who will be saved and leaves the rest to be damned. Cowper felt that he was not worthy to be classified as belonging to the chosen. He thought that, for whatever reason, election excluded him from the wonders of God's love.

Apparently he did not understand that we can find out whether we are one of the chosen! We can do this by coming to Christ and receiving His love and grace. If we do this, it is proof that God is at work drawing us to Himself. Notice how Christ combines God's sovereign work of election with the assurance that those who come to Him will be received. "All that the Father gives Me shall come to Me; and the one who comes to Me I will certainly not cast out" (John 6:37). Cowper could have taken comfort from the fact that the gospel is offered to all men.

No one who wishes to receive God's grace in Christ will ever be excluded. Indeed, "whoever will call upon the name of the Lord will be saved" (Romans 10:13). If only Cowper had grasped that grace was available for him since he desired to believe. As the preacher Spurgeon said with considerable insight, "He who worries about not being among the elect, probably is one of the elect!"

Receive Encouragement from Others

Often people who experience doubt are encouraged to know that others, often great men of the past, have doubted. It is not just the Cowpers of the world who have struggled with belief. Some biblical heroes have done so too.

John the Baptist, that great preacher of righteousness, was thrown into a dungeon for telling King Herod that he had an illegal marriage. The suffering turned John the prophet into John the doubter.

Why the doubts? First, he was suffering from injustice. His crime was speaking the truth to a king who needed to hear what God thought of his lifestyle. It is always difficult for us to reconcile God's love for us with a feeling of betrayal when we are wrongly accused. Our sense of fairness cries out for retribution. This is the soil in which our doubts grow.

Second, John was in isolation, solitary confinement. He did have some visitors, but nothing is more demoralizing than to survive when we cannot be strengthened by those who could stand with us in our need.

Third, and most important, his imprisonment seemed to be a breach of God's promise. He interpreted some Old Testament passages to teach that the Messiah would deliver the Israelites from the heavy-handed political occupation of Rome. The prisons would be opened, the enemy vanquished, and the nation of Israel freed.

Just the other day I inadvertently tore the flap from an envelope I hoped to mail. To find the missing piece, I went through my wastebasket, searching for the flap that would match the torn envelope. Just so, John could not find the missing piece. Reality did not square with the promises.

So John sent a group of disciples to Christ, asking him candidly, "Are You the Coming One, or shall we look for someone else?" (Matthew 11:3 NKJV). He was being as polite as he could be, but the question could not have been more pointed or plaintive. He was wondering whether the Christ had been mistakenly identified.

Christ did not chide John for wavering. Nor did He preach a sermon about the evils of unbelief. He pointed John to the Scriptures. First, He said, in effect, that prophecy *was* being fulfilled: "Go and report to John what you hear and see: the blind receive sight and the lame walk, the lepers are cleansed and the deaf hear, and the dead are raised up, and the poor have the gospel preached to them. And blessed is he who keeps from stumbling over Me" (Matthew 11:4–6).

Yes, some Scriptures *were* being fulfilled, even if others were not. John, like most of his peers, did not realize that there would be two comings of the Messiah, separated by hundreds of years. Yes, Christ *will* return to bring about the political deliverance the Old Testament promised, but that was not to happen now. John was insisting on present fulfillment of a promise that was to be fulfilled in the future.

Second, Christ added, "Blessed is he who keeps from stumbling over Me" (verse 6). Christ was saying that those who would believe even when He was not fulfilling their expectations would be blessed. Yes, there were reasons why some might stumble because of Him, but those who believed, even when disappointed, would be blessed.

It is interesting that it was in the context of his doubt that Christ proclaimed the greatness of John the Baptist: "Truly, I say to you, among those born of women there has not arisen anyone greater than John the Baptist; yet he who is least in the kingdom of heaven is greater than he" (Matthew 11:11). F. B. Meyer says of this, "The Master seems to say, heaven judges, not by a passing mood but by the general tenor of a man's life." With that, John is beheaded and passes from this life to the next.

And what shall we say of the disciple Thomas? He had a streak of pessimism, the sense that in the end nothing would come out quite right. It happened that Thomas was absent the day Christ appeared to the other disciples in the Upper Room. When the disciples saw Thomas, they shouted, "We have seen the Lord!" Thomas should have believed, for he had the report of these ten credible witnesses. What is more, he had known Christ and was privy to the miracles He had performed.

But Thomas replied, "Unless I shall see in His hands the imprint of the nails, and put my finger into the place of the nails, and put my hand into His side, I will not believe" (John 20:25). Eight days later Christ graciously gave Thomas his request. Thomas had the honesty to admit the truth when the evidence was convincing. He exclaimed, "My Lord and My God!"

Let me encourage you by saying that your name might just be in the Bible. Christ said to Thomas, "Because you have seen Me, have you believed? Blessed are they who did not see, and yet believed" (verse 29). We could paraphrase it, "Blessed are you, Tom, Ruth, or Marie, for, though you have not seen, you have believed!"

Who but a doubting Cowper could write of God:

Behind a frowning providence
He hides a smiling face.

His life should be an encouragement to all who doubt.

LESSONS FOR STRENGTHENING FAITH

Several years ago I interviewed a young minister who later died of a rare, fast-growing brain tumor. The doctors had told him he had only a few months to live, so he did all that he could to prepare his peers for the future success of his ministry.

"When the electricity goes off," he told me, "you can walk around in the darkness of your house because you lived in it when it was light." Then he added, "I want to walk with God in the light so that when the darkness comes, I will know my way around." Months later, he died with resignation and acceptance, knowing that even in the darkness he could trust the faithfulness of God. The better we know God in the light, the better we will be prepared for the dark.

We can grow in our faith if we remember these principles.

First, *faith does not exclude doubt.* Whether John the Baptist, Job, or Peter, who walked on the water, these believed despite their doubts. The father of the son stricken by convulsions (Mark 9:20) reflected the ambivalence of us all when he cried, "Lord, I believe; help thou mine unbelief" (verse 24 KJV).

Luther said, "Faith is the free surrender and a joyous wager on the unseen, untried and unknown goodness of God." Someday our faith will become sight. Until then, we might tremble on the rock of God's promises, even though the rock beneath us remains unshaken.

Second, *doubts might lead to certainties.* A seventeenth-century philosopher said, "If a man will begin with certainties he will end in doubts; but if he is content to begin with doubts, he will end in certainties." Or perhaps we should change that and say that doubts should end with certainties. Doubt can be used by God to deepen our faith by showing us how far we yet have to progress in our Christian experience. Our faithlessness, says Paul, in no way changes God's faithfulness (see 2 Timothy 2:13).

New believers often have an overwhelming sense of God's presence. He seems as near to them as breath itself. With time, those feelings dissipate so that we might learn to believe His bare word, even without the spiritual ecstasy we once experienced.

Doubts make our faith even more precious to God. The faith by which we believe in Christ is a gift of God, granted to those whom God has chosen for eternal life. But growth in faith is the constant theme of the New Testament. It is precisely because we are so prone to doubt that "the proof of your faith, being more precious than gold which is perishable, even though tested by fire, may be found to result in praise and glory and honor at the revelation of Jesus Christ" (1 Peter 1:7). Our doubts might, in the end, purify our faith.

Third, *admitting our doubts to others, and particularly to God, is essential.* God already knows our doubts, of course, but allowing us to admit them is His way of helping us in our need. For example, in Psalm 13 David remembers the times when he felt close to God, and that helps him to overcome his fear that God has forsaken him.

> How long, O Lord? Wilt Thou forget me forever? How long wilt Thou hide Thy face from me? How long shall I take counsel in my soul, having sorrow in my heart all the day? How long will my enemy be exalted over me? Consider and answer me, O Lord, my God; enlighten my eyes, lest I sleep the sleep of death, lest my enemy say, "I have overcome him," lest my adversaries rejoice when I am shaken. But I have trusted in Thy lovingkindness; my heart shall rejoice in Thy salvation. I will sing to the Lord, because He has dealt bountifully with me. (Psalm 13:1–6)

In Bunyan's famous allegory *The Pilgrim's Progress,* the men Christian and Hopeful disobey their instructions when they leave the path toward the Celestial City and climb over a giant fence. There they encounter a terrifying storm. They are caught by Giant Despair and thrust into the dungeon called Doubting Castle. Here they languish until Christian realizes he has the key of God's promises that will bring release and restoration. And so it is. Assurance cannot come by looking at our good deeds but by looking to the promises of Christ.

Suppose the sun is shining outside, but you are in a darkened room. The shutter in front of you is preventing the sun from bringing light within. You are not being asked to generate the light and heat of the sun. That has already been done. Your only task, the one you *must* do, is to open the shutter and come to Christ with the helpless recognition that He alone is able to save you.

If Cowper was a believer, as we have reason to believe, he lacked assurance because he simply could not see the grace of God. Though most Christians have more faith than doubts, Cowper had more doubts than faith. Thanks be, the object of his wavering faith was Christ. Better to have little faith in Christ than solid faith in our good works or other means of grace. Too bad he could not throw the shutter open!

One day a man in great distress called me to say that he was terrified that he was not a Christian, believing that he was eternally damned and simply unable to believe. This modern-day Cowper kept grace at arm's length, insisting that he had "tried to believe" but found it impossible.

He thought he had to resolve all of his doubts before he could come to Christ. I explained that he could come to Christ as he was, doubts and all. Whatever little faith he had must be put in the only One who is able to save him.

But when I asked him to pray with me, he hung up, saying, "I'm not ready to come to Christ." I don't know why he was unwilling to come to Christ with his doubts. I should think that someone who was troubled about his eternal soul would be glad to come with his needs.

Could it be that the real reason was that he simply did not want to believe, despite his despair? Despite his confessed desire to be saved, he appeared to be a volitional doubter, a man who for all his emotional guilt nevertheless chose not to believe. And if he does not believe, he will not be saved.

Another man called me with the same kind of troubled spirit. He had sold his soul to the Devil and now felt he needed to honor his promise. He even doubted whether Christ was actually stronger than Satan and could therefore deliver him from his bondage.

I urged him to come to Christ, just as he was, doubts and all. To come with little faith is better than to not come at all. To come hesitantly is better than turning away with wistful sorrow.

I quoted the words I share with all doubters, a beautiful stanza of Charlotte Elliot's famous hymn:

> *Just as I am, though tossed about*
> *With many a conflict, many a doubt,*
> *Fightings and fears within, without,*
> *O lamb of God I come! I come!*

The young man came to Christ with his doubts, accepting Christ as his sin-bearer. Though he since has had many struggles with the enemy, he discovered by faith that he had been accepted by God.

Unbelief will damn us; doubts do not. God receives honest doubters; He does not accept dishonest ones.

NOTES

1. Virginia Stem Owens, "The Dark Side of Grace," *Christianity Today,* 19 July 1993, 32–33.
2. Martin Luther, *What Luther Says: An Anthology,* ed. Ewald M. Plass (St. Louis: Concordia), 1:487.

$\mathscr{Y}$ES, ... BUT

If you have followed the discussion so far, you probably have many questions. Accepting God's grace is never easy, especially if you have been brought up with the notion that we are expected to earn our salvation. Or maybe you were told that eternal life is a free gift, but we are in constant danger of losing it if we don't perform.

Here are some of the most common questions I have been asked whenever I speak on the topic of salvation.

Question:
What about those passages that seem to teach that baptism is necessary for salvation?

Answer:
Although there are those who teach that without this ritual no one will ever be saved, our salvation is not dependent upon baptism.

Let us always remember that the Bible is consistent with itself. More than one hundred times we are told that faith in Christ establishes our relationship with God. If baptism were necessary, why would Paul say to the church in Corinth, "I thank God that I baptized none of you except Crispus and Gaius, that no man should say you were baptized in my name. Now I did baptize also the household of Stephanas; beyond that, I do not know whether I baptized any other. For Christ did not send me to baptize, but to preach the gospel, not in cleverness of speech, that the cross of Christ should not be made void" (1 Corinthians 1:14–17).

The apostle makes two points. First, although baptism is important, he wasn't called to baptize but to "preach the gospel." Second, it is clear that Paul distinguishes baptism and the gospel. Baptism does not save, but the gospel does. When Paul describes the gospel in 1 Corinthians 15:1–8, he does not mention baptism.

In addition to John 3:5, which was discussed in chapter 4 of this book, two other passages are often thought to teach that baptism is necessary for salvation. The first of these is Acts 2:38. On the day of Pentecost, Peter said, "Repent, and let each of you be baptized in the name of Jesus Christ for the forgiveness of your sins; and you shall receive the gift of the Holy Spirit."

The mention of both baptism and repentance in the same verse does not mean that both are necessary for the forgiveness of sins. I might say, "Take your keys and coat and start the car," but that does not mean that taking your coat is necessary to starting the car, even though it is mentioned along with taking the keys.

The Greek grammar of Acts 2:38 confirms this interpretation. The phrase "and let each of you be baptized in the name of Jesus Christ" is actually a parenthesis, and it is singular, which sets it off from the rest of the sentence.

The command to repent is plural, and so is the phrase "for the forgiveness of your sins." "Repent . . . for the forgiveness of your sins" is the central point. Notice also that in Acts 10:43, Peter mentions faith as the *only* requirement to receive the forgiveness of sins.

A second passage that some believe teaches baptism as the way of salvation was written by Peter: "And corresponding to that, baptism now saves you—not the removal of dirt from the flesh, but an appeal to God for a good conscience—through the resurrection of Jesus Christ" (1 Peter 3:21).

Peter makes a parallel between the waters that appear in the story of Noah and the ritual of baptism. Water did not save Noah at all but was actually an instrument of judgment. The ark saved him by bringing him "safely through the water" (verse 20 NASB; compare KJV, "saved by water").

Peter goes on to explain that water does not save *us,* either. Baptism saves, he says, but it is not the physical act of the washing that does it ("not the removal of dirt from the flesh") but rather "an appeal to God for a good conscience—through the resurrection of Jesus Christ" (verse 21).

What saves? The appeal of a good conscience before God. That word *appeal* can be translated "answer." The people at that time were required to make a statement of faith before being baptized, and this saved them from a guilty conscience.

Many people in Peter's day were afraid to confess Christ publicly for fear of being persecuted. Those who *did* publicly testify had made an appeal for a "good conscience."

To summarize the parallel: Water didn't save Noah, but he was brought safely through the water because of his faith in God. Nor does water save the person who is baptized, but his confession at the time of baptism saves him from a timid conscience.

Question:

There are some passages, for example Hebrews 6, that seem to teach that a believer can fall away into sin and be lost forever. How should these passages be interpreted?

Answer:

True believers cannot fall away to eternal damnation.

Since whole books have been written about these matters, I will respond to only one of the controversial passages.

In Hebrews 6, the author wrote that in the case of those who have begun the Christian life and then have fallen away, "it is impossible to renew them again to repentance" since "they again crucify to themselves the Son of God, and put Him to open shame" (verses 4–6)

We have to admit that the author is talking about true Christians in this passage, for his description of these people is clear (see Hebrews 6:1–3). Not all commentators agree with this interpretation, but, if you read the context, it makes the best sense.

Yes, believers can "fall away." But does that mean to be lost in hell forever? The context makes clear that this is not what the writer had in mind. He used the same expression "fall away" for the Israelites who fell in the desert (3:17; cf. verse 12). Their "falling away" did not determine their eternal destiny but resulted in earthly chastisement and loss of temporal blessings.

The book of Hebrews was written to those who were tempted to revert to the Old Testament sacrificial system. They were beginning to doubt whether Christ was fully sufficient, whether He did in fact replace the rituals and sacrifices required by the law. To have such doubts indicated unbelief and hardness of heart. To return to the Old Testament sacrifices was to "again crucify to themselves the Son of God, and put Him to open shame" (Hebrews 6:6).

The point is that so long as they were returning to the Old Testament sacrifices, they could not be brought back to repentance. Understandably, they could not be restored to fellowship with God *while* they were offering lambs on the altar ("since they again crucify to themselves the Son of God" NASB; "crucifying Christ afresh" KJV). But if they ceased such practices, there is no reason to suggest that they could not be restored. Yes, believers can fall away, but not to eternal damnation.

Question:
What about passages such as Revelation 3:5, where we read that those who overcome will not have their names erased from the book of life? Doesn't this imply that some people's names will be blotted out?

Answer:
No, it does not.

First, we should notice that the passage is a promise that Christ will *not* blot out the names of the faithful. Of course there is the implication that under certain circumstances He would blot out a name, but that is making an unnecessary assumption.

Bible scholars say that expressing a positive promise by using a negative is a *litotes,* that is, a figure of speech in which one thing is strongly affirmed by negating its opposite.

A good example of this is seen in John 6:37, where Jesus says, "All that the Father gives me will come to me,

and whoever comes to me I will never drive away": (NIV).
What Jesus means is that He will welcome those who
come to Him. Far from driving them away, He will keep
them and preserve them. We should not interpret this passage to mean that under certain circumstances He *does*
drive out those whom the Father has given Him.

Similarly, it makes no more sense to ask under what
condition Christ would blot a name from the book of life
than to ask under what condition He might drive away
those who come to Him. None of those who belong to
Christ will be blotted out.

Question:

What about those passages that teach that if we deny
Christ He will deny us? Does this not show that unless we
live up to our end of the bargain we will lose our salvation?

Answer:

Most Christians do not deny Christ, at least permanently.
That is why there have been so many martyrs throughout
the history of the Christian church. But if a true believer
should deny Christ, that does not mean that he will lose
his salvation. Christ will never deny that a child is His,
although He may well deny a child a place of honor in
the kingdom.

God gives His people the grace to stand for Him even
in the midst of much opposition. However, some Bible
teachers have pushed this point to an extreme and interpret such passages to teach that no true believer ever
denies Christ. They hold that all believers may have occasional lapses but will always progress toward a deep-
er commitment to Christ. So, the argument goes, if you
really deny Christ you were never truly saved.

I respectfully disagree. History has shown that many true Christians denied Christ during times of persecution. And if we were honest, we too can deny Him through our silence or maybe even through our words, as Peter did in the presence of a servant girl the night before the crucifixion (see John 18:15, 25–27). Most of the time Christians bounce back from such failures, but I think we would be naive to think that no true believer has ever lived and died in a state of denial of Christ.

I think, however, that we are too quick to assume that Christ's denial of those who deny Him means that they will be eternally lost. In fact, the very context of 2 Timothy 2:11–13 speaks of God's faithfulness toward us in the midst of our failure. We read, "It is a trustworthy statement: For if we died with Him, we shall also live with Him; if we endure, we shall also reign with Him; if we deny Him, He also will deny us; if we are faithless, He remains faithful; for He cannot deny Himself."

Obviously, Paul believed that we Christians could become "faithless," though that would not alter God's faithfulness toward us. A failure to endure would mean, rather, that we cannot reign with Him, because such a privilege is given only to those who are faithful in this life.

So a failure to endure is a form of denial, and, appropriately, if we deny Him, He will deny us. He would not deny that we are His children (for He is faithful to His promises), but He will deny us a special reward and place of honor in the kingdom. This is illustrated by the servant in Luke 19:22–24, who did not hear the "well done," nor was he allowed to reign with Christ, though his soul was saved. Yes, in the end, everyone in heaven will be fulfilled, but some will be given a more prominent position than others.

We also read that Christ will be ashamed of us if we are ashamed of Him (Mark 8:38). This does not refer to a loss of eternal life but to a loss of honor and recognition in the presence of Christ. That explains why John says we should live in such a way that we will not be ashamed before Him at His coming (1 John 2:28; see also Mark 8:38). Shame is always experienced in direct proportion to sensitivity to sin. When we are transformed and see sin for what it really is, when we "know even as we are known" (see 1 Corinthians 13:12), we might be ashamed indeed.

Question:
Doesn't the doctrine of eternal security lead to a wanton lifestyle? If people know that they are saved eternally, will they not have no motivation to keep their relationship with God current?

Answer:
There is always the possibility that we will misuse grace. However, the believer has been regenerated by the Holy Spirit and has received a radical transformation. Believers who do misuse grace will experience God's discipline.

Paul had to warn the believers in Galatia that they were not to misuse their freedom. Grace is vulnerable to misuse. However, two things must be borne in mind.

First, those who have been regenerated by the Holy Spirit have experienced a radical transformation. The Holy Spirit changes the inner desires and disposition of those who believe so that they are given a new appetite and a new spiritual motivation.

Of course, there might be backsliding and struggles with sin, for believers are, as Luther has said, "simultaneously saint and sinner." But there is a change in our affections. We now love God, whereas before we regarded Him with indifference.

Second, when we become one of God's children, He begins to discipline us for disobedience. God does not let His children "get by" with their rebellion. Sometimes the discipline is through circumstances; sometimes it is by internal despair.

I am told that a Christian woman once said to her pastor, "Well, for the Christian, sin is different than it is for the non-Christian." To which the pastor replied, "You are right; for the Christian it is more serious!"

Question:
Did not James say that we are justified by works and not faith only? Why are you so insistent that we are justified by faith alone?

Answer:
Both Paul and James taught that Abraham was justified by faith alone.

Some people think that James taught that Abraham was justified by faith *and* works because he wrote, "Was not Abraham our father justified by works, when he offered up Isaac his son on the altar? You see that faith was working with his works, and as a result of the works, faith was perfected" (James 2:21–22). They contrast this with Paul, who said, "If Abraham was justified by works, he has something to boast about; but not before God" (Romans 4:2).

James is consistent with Paul because the two of them are using the word *justification* with different meanings. Paul is talking about our justification in the sight of God; James is speaking about our justification in the sight of others. He uses the word *justification* in the sense I might if I asked, "Can you justify your belief in God?"

We know that James had this meaning of justification in mind because of the difference in time between two important events in Abraham's life. In Genesis 15:6, God renews the covenant with him, and Abraham "believed in the Lord; and he counted it to him for righteousness" (KJV). This is the justification of which Paul speaks.

Years later, when Abraham was willing to offer Isaac on the altar, his original faith was vindicated. That, says James, is when he was "justified by works." This was the fulfillment of his original faith.

As a result of Abraham's obedience in the test regarding Isaac (see Genesis 22), he could now be called a "friend of God" (James 2:23; cf. 2 Chronicles 20:7; Isaiah 41:8). Future generations saw his act as a proof that indeed he loved God above everything else. Had he not obeyed God in his willingness to offer Isaac on the altar, he still would have been justified by faith before God (see Genesis 14, 15, 16, and 17). But by passing the test of obedience in Genesis 22, his faith was vindicated and he attained special recognition among men.

We must bear in mind that the word *justification* is often used in the sense of *vindication* in other contexts (for example, in Matthew 12:37). We ourselves use the word *justify* in other contexts, just as did the biblical writers.

A FINAL APPEAL

Sometimes nursery rhymes are more than just a bit of doggerel:

Humpty Dumpty sat on a wall
Humpty Dumpty had a great fall
All the kings horses
And all the kings men
Couldn't put Humpty together again

This poem might have been written to describe a politician in England, but it is a parable about us. We have had a great fall; the evidence is all around us. We simply cannot put ourselves back together again. Much less can we reconcile ourselves with God. Only Christ can put our lives back together by spanning the chasm that exists between us and God.

Many good people will be in hell because they put faith in their goodness. Others will die believing that they had sinned too greatly to be saved. No wonder "the way is broad that leads to destruction and many are those who enter by it."

The question is neither the greatness of our sin nor the long list of good things we have done; the question is whether we have placed our trust in Christ alone, persuaded that He has done all that is necessary and ever will be necessary for us to be welcomed by God.

An old man stood to his feet in a church service and said, "It has taken me fifty-two years to learn three things."

The congregation hushed, hoping to discover in three minutes what had taken this man so long to learn.

"First," he began, "I learned that I cannot save myself. Second, I learned that God did not expect me to save myself."

Then he lowered his voice and added, "And the third thing I've learned is that God, through Christ, has done it all!"

And so it is. For those who are willing to entrust their eternal souls into Christ's care, for them, God has done it all.

I have written a prayer that I would encourage you to pray, though I must caution you that it is not the prayer itself that will save you. Only Christ can do that. What's important is that this prayer be simply the desire that is in your heart. If you pray it in faith, Christ will save you. Christ will respond to the faith in your heart. Don't back away, for He has promised that He will receive all who come to Him.

O God,

I know that I have sinned and that I cannot save myself. I thank You that Christ died to reconcile me to You. At this moment I accept Him as my sin-bearer. I affirm that His death was for me; I receive His sacrifice in my behalf.

I receive from You at this moment what I do not have. I take the gift of eternal life, which You have promised to those who believe. As best I can, I now transfer all of my trust to Christ.

Thank You for hearing this prayer in the name of Jesus Christ the Lord.

Amen.

"Truly, truly I say to you, he who hears My word, and believes on Him who sent Me, has eternal life, and does not come into judgment, but has passed from death into life" (John 5:24).

"The one who believes in the Son of God has the witness in himself; the one who does not believe God has made Him a liar, because he has not believed the witness that God has borne concerning His Son" (1 John 5:10).

Thanks be to God, who has given us assurance that we will spend eternity with Him.

Soli Deo Gloria.